FIFTY FABULOUS YEARS
1945 – 1995
A Pictorial History of The City of Santa Maria and Santa Maria Valley, California

Santa Maria Times Photo

Jim May, Editor

Published by *Curtis Media, Inc.*

Co-Publishers:

S&S Enterprises (Floyd Snyder)

Hacienda National Bank

ISBN: 0-88107-268-0

Copyright © Curtis Media, Inc.—1997

To obtain copies of this book contact S&S Enterprises, P.O. Box 922, Santa Maria, CA, 93456, (805) 922-9791.

To obtain information on how to publish your own county or community history, contact:

Curtis Media, Inc.

1-800-743-4388

BOOK SPONSORS

AGRO-JAL FARMS, INC.
DENNIS BETHEL & ASSOCIATES
COAST ROCK
CUSTOM COLORS
A.J. DIANI FAMILY
DUDLEY HOFFMAN MORTUARY
MARIAN MEDICAL CENTER
ROEMERS
SANTA MARIA VALLEY RAILROAD CO.
SHEEHY BERRY FARMS
SOUTHERN CALIFORNIA GAS CO.

ENDORSEMENTS:

We are Extremely grateful that a number of important local organizations, both governmental and private, gave us their backing from this project's inception. They endorsed, encouraged and assisted this photo history of our valley. These are:

SANTA MARIA CITY COUNCIL

SANTA BARBARA COUNTY BOARD OF SUPERVISORS

SANTA MARIA VALLEY CHAMBER OF COMMERCE

SANTA MARIA VALLEY ECONOMIC DEVELOPMENT ASSN.

SANTA MARIA VALLEY PIONEER ASSN.

SANTA MARIA VALLEY BEAUTIFUL

SANTA MARIA VALLEY HISTORICAL SOCIETY

THIS BOOK IS DEDICATED TO:

Jacqueline Argonne May

My wife, Jacqueline Argonne May.
Without her patience,
forebearance, support and loving
encouragement this book
would never have been completed.

Special thanks to Floyd Snyder of **S&S Enterprises** and **Strictly Business Magazine.** His unstinting support with staff, facilities and sound advice have been critical in coping with the many difficulties in completing this book.

Floyd A. Snyder

ACKNOWLEDGEMENTS

FIFTY FABULOUS YEARS could not have been created without the generous donation or loan of thousands of photographs by hundreds of people. Photo credit notations name those whose pictures are used in this book. We are extremely grateful to them and to all of the others who entrusted their treasured photographs to us for consideration.

We give special thanks to Mrs. Georgia Moore, widow of the late Robert Moore, for loaning her entire collection of thousands of negatives of photographs taken here in our valley by Mr. Moore during the 1940's and 50's. We are also indebted to Douglas Coleman for his dedicated work and consummate skill in producing high quality enlargements from hundreds of these historic negatives. These photographs are marked in the book as "(Moore/Coleman Photo)".

We also wish to thank the many people of our valley who were kind enough to help us in our efforts to locate photographs or to track down information about individual pictures.

Advance purchasers of "Fifty Fabulous Years" and lenders of photographs have been remarkably patient and forebearing during the more than three years that have elapsed since the book was first announced and orders taken. We are profoundly grateful for their endurance and trust while our project completion date was repeatedly (but unavoidably) delayed.

To everybody who helped with the book in any way we say "Thank You! Thank You! Thank You!"

James A. "Jim" May
Project Director

FOREWORD

This picture book is designed to help bring the history of Santa Maria Valley up-to-date. It supplements the two excellent earlier histories published by the Santa Maria Valley Historical Association: "This is our Valley" in 1959, and "Santa Maria Historic Photo Album" in 1987. These deal with Valley history up through World War II. Other local specialized histories of great merit, which include interesting historic photographs and facts, include: "G. Allan Hancock" by DeWitt Meredith 1964 (a privately published limited edition) "Old Town Orcutt" by Bob Nelson 1987, "From Boom Town to Bedroom Community" by Sally L. Simon 1990, "My Town-Santa Maria California 1941-1945" by Milton E. Shriner 1991, and "San Ramon Chapel Pioneers and their California Heritage" by Erlinda Pertussi Ontiveros 1990, "Sagas of the Central Coast" Bob Nelson, Publisher 1994.

The book offers pictorial glimpses of some of the major (and minor) activities and changes that have occurred in our valley during the past fifty-plus years. It also highlights some of the many outstanding leaders and players that have catalyzed the remarkable tenfold growth in our population and the substantial improvement in our material wealth and quality of life that has characterized these years. Some subjects from earlier dates have been covered whenever it seemed useful in telling the story and photographs were available.

I have tried to present a balanced selection of photographs that illustrated some of the main aspects of life in Santa Maria Valley and the many changes that have occurred during these dynamic years. This has not worked out as well as I had hoped, due to the limitations of space and the non-availability of many important photographs. Many of the people, places and events that we would have liked to include were not to be found among the many thousands of photographs loaned or given to us.

It was very hard to select from among the many interesting photographs loaned to us. For lack of space we had to pick out a sampling and leave out many, many wonderful photographs, many important people and many exciting activities and key events. We regret these limitations, but have done our best.

This is a PICTURE history. And it is said that "a good picture is worth a thousand words". If so, this book is the equivalent of about a million words. I leave it to others, in the future, to actually put the history into words.

We have provided descriptive captions for most of our photographs, including the names of persons pictured — if known. We have avoided extensive descriptions of all that is to be seen in each photograph. We leave it to sharp-eyed "readers" to spot the interesting details, particularly "readers" who have lived in our town or valley during these fantastic and mostly happy years.

A final personal suggestion to everybody. PLEASE write the names, date, place, event and a few explanatory comments on the back of every photo you take or receive. A short time later you will remember little if anything about your unmarked photos. Nearly 90% of the photos we have seen while researching for this book had little or no information available. How sad! What a loss! Give yourself and your family a break. Give future historians a break. Please label those Photos!

James A. "Jim" May
Editor

INTRODUCTION

Fifty Fabulous Years of Change and Progress in Santa Maria Valley

A small handful of key political decisions initiated development projects in our valley that set the course for modernization, growth and an improved, but different, more complex quality of life. Among these critical decisions were:

1 — The construction of Twitchell Dam and levees on the Santa Maria River and at the outfall from Bradley Canyon. These put an end to the floods that had periodically devastated Santa Maria and many of its farms for nearly a century. The city became able to grow north across the former flood plain. AND the overdraft of the underground water supply, on which both towns and farms depend, was fully mitigated.

2 — The acquisition by local government of the huge Santa Maria Army Airfield south of town, shortly after the war. This enabled Santa Maria to resume its leading role in civil aviation on the central coast (as created by Capt. G. Allan Hancock in the 1920's and 30's), and to create a modern industrial park.

3 — The relocation of Highway 101 to bypass Santa Maria on the east. This solved the traffic problems on Broadway for many years and induced the growth of the city east to the new freeway and beyond. But Santa Maria lost its unique visual identity to 101 travelers, and many tourist-serving businesses on Broadway were dealt a mortal blow.

4 — The construction of the Army's Tank Training Center at Camp Cooke and its post-war conversion to Vandenberg Air Force Missile Base. While not the result of local decisions, these were powerful positive influences on the future of our valley. They brought high-paying jobs, contracts, and high quality people.

5 — Downtown Redevelopment changed the face of our town forever. Most of the old downtown structures were bulldozed into oblivion and replaced by a modern air-conditioned shopping mall, parking structures, Broadway Bridge, shopping centers and department stores. The wisdom and relative success of our redevelopment is still a matter of local controversy.

6 — The purchase of a 16,000 acre foot allotment of State Water provided assurance that Santa Maria's plans for steady growth over the next twenty years can be implemented safely. It further ensures that the quality of our drinking water will be vastly improved, beginning in 1996 when State Water is scheduled to arrive.

7 — The planned expansion of the City's Sphere of Influence and ultimate annexation of 3,100 acres of land (mostly marginal and south of town) provides for balanced and timely growth of business, industry, and housing to reach a population of about 100,000 over the next twenty years or more.

TABLE OF CONTENTS

GEORGE S. HOBBS CIVIC CENTER

The Santa Maria City Council in 1995 recognized former Mayor Hobbs' many years of service to the people of Santa Maria by designating the City's central buildings complex as the "GEORGE S. HOBBS CIVIC CENTER". Mr. Hobbs served on the City Council for 34 years from 1960 - 1994 and was Mayor for 22 years.

Left: The new George S. Hobbs Civic Center monument is located near Broadway centered on the walkway between City Hall and the Library.

Above: Mayor George S. Hobbs and his Wife Blanche — Photo Circa 1990.

EARLY MAPS OF SM VALLEY

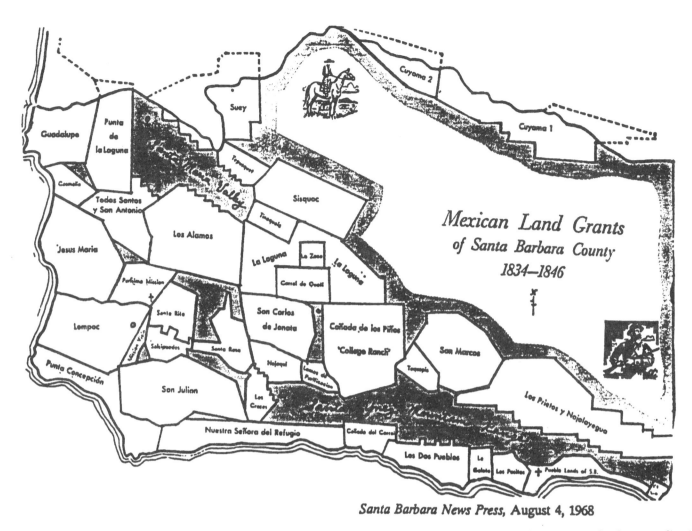

Santa Barbara News Press, August 4, 1968

This old map shows that most of SM Valley was not included in the Mexican land grants. As U.S. Govt. land it was opened to homesteading in the late 1860's.

Conceptual Relief Map showing Santa Maria Valley in the 1930's before Hiway 101 was moved east of town. Betteravia Lake still retained its original shape and size. (Photo courtesy Maurice Twitchell)

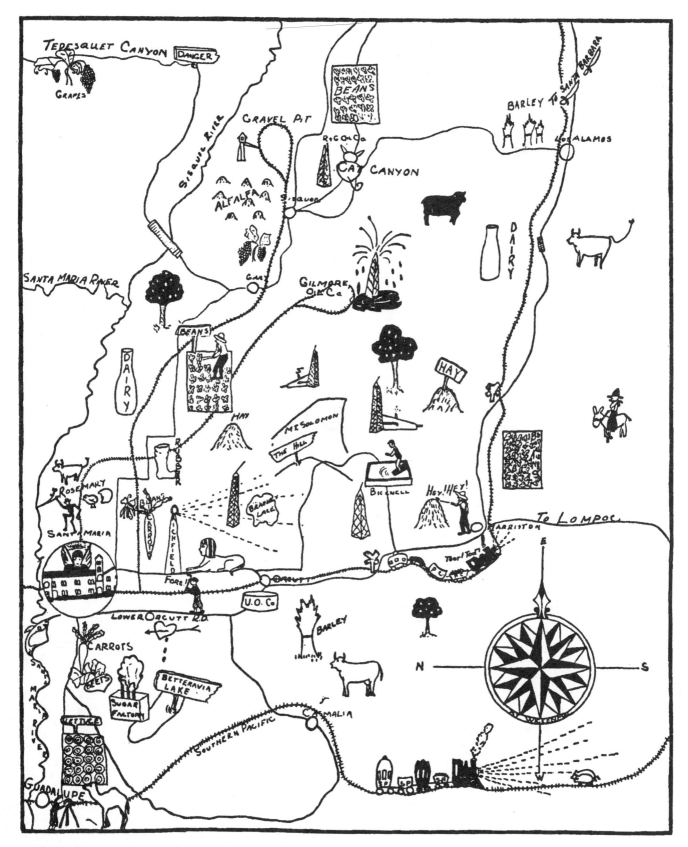

SANTA MARIA UNION HIGH SCHOOL DISTRICT

Sketch map of SM Valley from 1931 High School "Review". Symbols and labels locate important crops, activities and sites. Most of these are gone, with little traces remaining. Old Timers will have no trouble decoding the symbols.

SANTA MARIA — 1931

Air view north across city Sept. 23, 1931. Hancock Field bottom right. High School bottom left. (Photo by H.W. "Rudy" Truesdale. Courtesy of Harry Clark).

SANTA MARIA — 1955

Santa Maria — Looking north along Broadway (Hiway 101) April 17, 1955. Newlove Tract in right foreground. City Population about 15,000. (Photo courtesy Jeanett Sainz.

Santa Maria — Looking east along Main St. — March 4, 1956. (Photo courtesy Jeanett Sainz)

WONDERFUL WEATHER

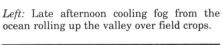

Left: Late afternoon cooling fog from the ocean rolling up the valley over field crops.

Above: Kite flying at beach on a typical sunny, breezy day. (*SM Times* Photo)

Left middle: Early morning fog obscures Broadway Bridge and Robinson-May bldg. View north on Broadway from Cook St.

Left: City Hall and E. Cook St. shrouded in morning fog

Afternoon cool ocean breezes also can kick up dust. Modern agricultural practices and urban landscaping and forests have virtually eliminated the historic dust nuisance.

Afternoon winds ripple flags all over town. These are at the War Veteran's Memorial at SM public cemetery.

Snow in the hills around the Valley is rare and short-lasting, occurring every 10 to 15 years. Snow on the floor of the valley occurs for a few hours only — several times in 100 years. Views are south and west from the top of the 7 story Union Plaza Senior hi-rise bldg. in 1989. (Photo courtesy Terry Krelle)

6

FLOODING IN TOWN — EARLY 1900'S

Broadway & Cypress.
(Photo courtesy Tommy Rice)

Cypress & Lincoln
(Photo by Frank Crakes)

Front yards under water — Cypress & Lincoln 1913-14. *L to R:* Homer Young, Clarence Crakes, Frank Crakes. (Photo courtesy C. Wright Crakes)

Downtown on a typical rainy day — early 1900's.
(Photo courtesy Tommy Rice)

Typical backyards under water. (Photo courtesy Tommy Rice)

300 block. So. Broadway, west side, flowing bank to bank with flood water from Bradley Canyon. (Photo by Frank Crakes)

400 block So. Broadway — Gladys Froom and Rex Hocker in Duck Boat — 1913-14 flood. (Photo by Frank Crakes)

Mill & warehouse marooned — Cor Mill & No. Smith streets.
(Photo courtesy Maurice Twitchell)

Miller Street — view north from highground of SMVRR tracks. St. Mary's Church Steeple at right background. (Photo by Frank Crakes)

7

DOWNTOWN FLOODING — THRU 1952

Residential area 400 block So. Broadway — note pepper trees — view NW. (Photo by Frank Crakes)

Routine annual flooding from Bradley Canyon at Broadway & Cook St. Circa 1943. Note pedestrian bridge from curb to high center of Cook St. Old Carnegie Library at Right. (A Moore/Colman photo)

W. Church St. from Broadway, circa 1920. Also afflicted by Bradley Canyon runoff. (Photo courtesy Maurice Twitchell)

Broadway & Cook — circa 1941. Methodist Church— background. Shell gas station and Weber Bread Truck are long gone. (Moore/Coleman Photo)

Bradley Rd. (ex- Nance Rd.) under water 4/8/44. Veiw No. from Stowell Rd. (Photo courtesy SMVRR)

W. Main & Blosser area flooding — Feb. 1962 — view NW across intersection. (Photo courtesy Maurice Twitchell)

North Broadway circa 1941.
(Photo courtesy Tommy Rice)

Snappy Ford V-8 in deep water just outside the city limits.at corner Blosser & Guadalupe Rd. Circa 1941. These main roads were often flooded by heavy winter rains.

RIVER BRIDGES AND FLOODS

Left: Pacific Coast Railway train crossing flooded by Santa Maria River 1905-6. This was first bridge across the river. Built 1882 for the train, it had ties instead of a roadbed and could not be used by horses, wagons or livestock. (Photo by Jeanett Sainz)

Left below: 1913-14 winter flooding washed out the RR bridge. Frank W. Crakes in center. View is to north. Bridge was promptly repaired and served RR 'til line was abandoned and scrapped in 1939. (Photo by Homer Young — Courtesy of Wright Crakes)

Above: Dismantling the steel superstructure after several spans collapsed and wooden piling supports for roadbed were deemed stronger and less expensive to replace. (Moore/Coleman photo)

Left: First auto and wagon bridge was steel cantileur type built around 1908 as a link in the coastal hiway — which passed due south through Santa Maria on Broadway, later designated State Hiway 101. (Photo Courtesy Tommy Rice)

Left: Remodeled bridge at left. Paved road running parallel across the river bottom is US 101. The bridge was only open for use when 101 was flooded, and had alternating single lane one way traffic. (Moore/Colman photo). This road is now Preisker Lane in front of Preisker Park.

WATER FLOOD WASHOUTS — KEY LOCAL BRIDGES AND RAIL LINES

Above: SMVRR Bradley Canyon Line washed out March 8, 1941. Bradley Canyon is the source of most of the runoff that flooded downtown Santa Maria until the branch levee was built in the 1960's. (Photo courtesy SMV Railroad.

Top left; Suey Bridge washout Feb. 1938. (Photo courtesy Water Conservation Dist.)

Left: Sisquoc River Bridge washout Feb. 1938. A near disaster was averted in the heavy 1995 flooding by emergency strengthening and temporarily restricting use of the bridge. (Photo courtesy SM Valley Water Conservation District)

Key political leaders meeting at Santa Maria Inn to plan Vaquero Dam (later renamed Twitchell Dam) solution to perennial valley flooding problems — early 1950's. *L-R:* County Supervisor Marion A. Smith and Mayor Curtis Tunnell, State Senators Claire Engel and Jack Hollister, *Santa Maria Times Editors* Joe Hagerman and Bill Misslin. (Photo Courtesy Marion Smith)

RIVER BRIDGES AND FLOODING PROBLEMS — 1952

Above: Hiway 101 — SM River bridges Jan. 16, 1952, view south. *L to R (center)* Machado Airfield, old steel bridge bypass, steel bridge, city dump (now Preisker Park), old Pacific Coast RR right of way. (Photo Courtesy SMVRR)

Below: Suey Crossing bridge and flooding Jan 16, 1952 — view SW. Triangular area is "Suey Park", location for many decades of SMV Roping and Riding Club. (Photo courtesy SMVRR)

CONTROLLING SM RIVER FLOODING

Above: Farm road and fence form levee — somewhat. (Photo courtesy Maurice Twitchell)

Below: Steel posts and wire provide better flood protection — except for the big ones. (Photo courtesy Maurice Twitchell)

Top: Twitchell (originally Vacquero) Dam reservoir empty — 1994 — its usual condition after the winter flood water is metered out to soak into the main SM Valley aquifer.

Above: Aerial View of Twitchell Reservoir and Dam— 1983. Nearly full, after several wet winters.

Below: View from Hiway 166.

Bottom: Twitchell Dam — main water outlet tunnel south into Cuyaman River.. Sandy Knott, Dam and Reservoir resident manager at right.

Above: Modern levees along SM River have earth core, rip rap facing and other amenities that provide protection from 400 year floods. View downstream.

Below: View upriver from So. bank levee near Suey Crossing. Levees opened several thousands acres of land near river to safe urban development, and protect many thousands of acres of land from flooding and erosion

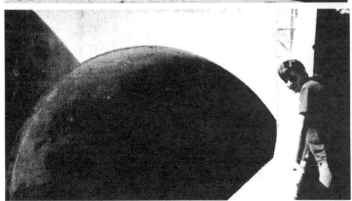

Top: High flood water in 1966 demonstrated the effectiveness of the new dam, levees and bridges. View from north end of bridge to south. (Photo by Merv Slawson)

Middle: North half of the twin bridges during the dry season in 1993.

Above: South half of twin bridges.

Left: Aerial view of twin bridges. (*Santa Maria Times* Photo)

HISTORIC HOMES SURVIVING

George Washington Battles' farm house — on Rosemary Rd. built 1869.

Charles William Smith ranch house on S. Bradley Rd. Built 1871 — sold to Enos Family around the turn of the century. Located on escarpment N. of Betteravia Rd.

Left: Adams (later Baker & Van Nelson house). 600 Blk. W. Mill St. — built 1879.

Lower left: Wm. C. Oakley house. 323 W. Mill St. — built 1903.

Corner left: Warren B. Rice house. Built circa 1905. Cor. W Orange and Pine Sts.

Paul Bradley ranch house — in Bradley Cyn. off Dominion Rd. Built 1888. (Photo courtesy Dick Bradley)

Alvin Cox farm house — now 1015 W. Donovan Rd. Built circa 1900.

John & Maria Newlove Country Mansion. Built 1906 about 3/4 mile south of town. House and palm trees moved to Ikola Historic Park in 1980's on commanding site above Hiway 101 as shown in photo.

Bradley Hotel (Originally The Hart House) built 1886 — burned down 1970. SE cor Bdwy. and Main St. — circa 1920. (Photo courtesy Floyd Snyder)

California Hotel (now Central City Hotel) built 1920's. First 3 story building. 200 blk No. Bdwy.

built circa 1880. Cor. W. Main and

Fuji Court — W. Main — circa 1950. (Photo courtesy Bob & Nancy De Armond)

Miyoshi Hotel — W. Main St. — circa 1950 (Photo courtesy Bob & Nancy De Armond)

rca 1940. Note indian stone bowls on le Kelly)

"New" motels (since WWII)

. Main St. Built early 1920's.

Rick's Drive-In Restaurant, BBQ and Motel — circa 1960 — cor. W. Bdwy & Donavan Rd. (Photo courtesy Laurel Hogle Kelly)

APARTMENTS AND GARDEN COURTS

Cook St. Apartments — opposite City Hall — in 1942 — Army vehicles in front were for removing trees for planting at Camp Cooke. (Moore/Colman Photo)

600 blk S. Curryer Apts. (Photo courtesy Bob & Nancy De Armond)

Buena Vista Court. One of first in town. 600 blk E. Church St. (Photo courtesy Bob & Nancy De Armond)

Mission Court — 600 blk E. Church St. (Photo courtesy Bob & Nancy De Armond)

Right: 114 W. Mill St — board and batten single wall construction. Built About 1900. (Photo courtesy Bob & Nancy De Armond)

Right: 114 W. Mill St — built about 1910. (Photo courtesy Bob & Nancy De Armond)

Right: Santa Maria's first modern 2 story stucco apt. house. (Photo courtesy Bob & Nancy De Armond)

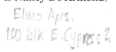

Elmo Apts. 100 blk E. Cypress 2.

Right: Union Plaza — 7 story — senior hi-rise apts.— built 1975 as part of "Saloon Row" redevelopment.

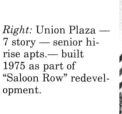

Right: Union Plaza sign. Union staff members. *L to R:* Terry Krelle, Pete Maratas.

DOWNTOWN

Above: 1910 — Center of town — view N. from Main St. — no flagpole. (Photo courtesy Dick Weldon)

Below: 1919 — Center of town — view N. from Church St. Flagpole honoring WWI Vets. erected ~~same~~ *1918* year. (Photo courtesy Fred Oakley May)

Above: Houk Building — Lodge meetings upstairs — W.B. Johnson Chevrolet right downstairs. Barron-Ames Milkshake shop at left. (Photo courtesy Bob & Nancy De Armond)

Above: 1942 city officials measuring for removal of flagpole — moved to city hall to facilitate military traffic on Hiway 101 thru town. City Engineer York Peterson second from left. (Moore/Colman photo)

Below: 1946 — "Whiskey Row" on 100 blk *East* W. Main St. (Photo courtesy RH Tesene)

Below: Bradley Hotel (former Hart House) largest structure downtown for over 50 years.

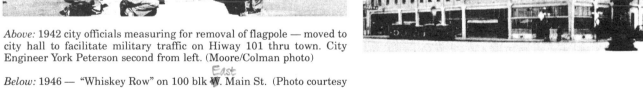

AROUND TOWN

Above: Dudley Mortuary cor. Lincoln and Church Sts. Theatre at rear. (Photo courtesy Bob & Nancy De Armond)

Left: Downtown 1960 — Broadway view No. from Rubel Bldg. (Photo courtesy Merv Slawson)

Above: Bianchi's Fruit Market Circa 1930. (Photo courtesy Ted Bianchi)

Left: 1925 Santa Maria Milk Co. & delivery trucks — W. Main St.

Below left: 1995 Santa Maria Glass Co.— with delivery trucks. (same building). (Photo courtesy Dale Iliff)

100 blk W. Main St. — 1995

View So. on N. Bdwy — circa 1950. (Moore/Coleman Photo)

Saladin Bldg. 700 S. Bdwy.

18

FIRST WHISKERINO CONTEST

1-Boyd Thomas
2-Ace. Krause
3-Hank Smith
4-Fred Filippani
5-Henry Elkins

6-Trueman Billings
7-Sam Niias
8-Archie Allan
9-Dave Contario
10-Jimmy Gray

11-Fred Buzzini
12-Johnny LaSaya
13-Chas Grisingher
14-Taylor Hopkins
15-Red Harris

16-Amil Jones
17-Joe Anderson
18-Winis Merrilum
20-Guy Raparto
20-Lou Schmaltz

21-Kenny Adam
22-Del Gruber
23-Jocko Knotts
24-Red Kamp
25-Tony Nunez

26-Joe Marcial
27-Buck Hartman
28-Al Pico
29-Alfred Vicente
30-Chick Inman

31-Percy Johnson
32-Owen Cowden
33-Ben Radisdnik
34-Don Donovan
35-Frank Brumalla

36-Mario DeBernardi
37-Brawly Herrera
38-Mr. Foster

First Whiskerino in Santa Maria — 1937. An annual contest during Elks Rodeo Week since 1940's. (Photo courtesy Nancy & Jack Stewart)

PARADES DOWN BROADWAY — 1940's & 1950's

Above: Bea Thomas Vallozza — cowgirl 1940's. (Photo courtesy Bea Vallozza)

Below: Joe A. Thomas — rancher. (Photo courtesy Beatrice Vallozza)

Mounted Gray Family members, color bearers in Elks Parade for many years. *L-R:* Joe, Joni, Dorothy and Norma. During 1950's. (Photo courtesy Joe Gray).

Above: Flagship Santa Maria by Knights of Columbus — circa 1940. (Moore/Colman Photo)

Above right: De Molay Patriots float. (Moore/Colman Photo)

Campfire Girls circa 1940. (Moore/Colman Photo) 1941 Ford Sedan!

Above: World Peace and Four Freedoms (Moore/Colman Photo)

Below: Rainbow Girls Assembly #92. (Moore/Colman Photo)

Below: "HooseGow" — local youth having fun. (Moore/Colman Photo)

Below: VFW barn dance float promoting fund-raising BBQ at Nojoqui Falls and Wed. nite Jr. Hi dances at Vets Memorial Bldg. (Moore/Colman Photo)

20

DINING OUT — POPULAR EATERIES

US Grill — 100 blk Bdwy — estab. 1917 by M.N. Firfires. Note Penny-operated scale at left. (Photo courtesy Floyd Snyder)

Santa Maria Inn — estab. 1917 by Frank McCoy. Note hallmark flowers in windows.

Santa Maria Club entrance 1935 — with city's first FBI agent Bill Nolan — temporary resident. (Photo courtesy Bill Nolan)

International Cafe in W. Main St. shopping area known to some as "Jap Town". (Photo courtesy Bob & Nancy De Armond)

Rick's Drive-In and Restaurant. Cor Broadway & Donovan Rd. in 1950's. Rural type mailbox and absence of sidewalk shows edge of town location at the time.

Ranch House Restaurant — About a mile So. of town on Coast Hiway. Camp Cooke Army Unit party around 1943. (Moore/Coleman Photo)

Leo's Drive In, No. Bdwy. (Photo courtesy Leo Dettamante)

The Boys Restaurant — 100 blk. N. College Ave.

Original Quito's Restaurant — 100 blk. E. Jones St. (Photo courtesy Rudy Rodriguez)

The renowned Far Western Restaurant. Estab. 1954 in Guadalupe. Co-owner Richard Maretti points to historic plaque. (*SM Times* Photo)

DINING OUT — POPULAR EATERIES

Above: Mr & Mrs. Burns Rick in new delivery truck at their popular drive in restaurant in 1950's. (Photo courtesy Mrs. Maxine Rick)

Above: Landmark Square Restaurant — 1995.

Right: Bronze historic marker at the Landmark.

Above: Birthday cake at Santa Maria Inn. Marian Hancock and Bill Nolan share birth-date of June 21, and 1991 celebration with friends. (Photo courtesy Bill Nolan)

Right: McDonald's 1950's king-size Golden Arches on S. Broadway are among the few preserved in the face of downsizing regulatory trends.

Below: Stag banquet at Santa Maria Club in the 1940's. Among those present can be seen: Buster Melschau, Chris Melschau, Peter Melschau, Carl Jenson, Olin Witaker, Chas. Careaga, Durward Careaga, Louis Cossa, Hans Melschau Sr., Hans Melschau Jr. Waiters include Elmer Griset and Charles Rusconi. (Photo courtesy John D. Bartel)

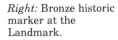

NEIGHBORHOOD MARKETS & GROCERY STORES

Left: Davidson's Grocery 1924, corner of Lincoln and Orange St. Davidson Family *L-R:* Marshall, Gracie, James, Will, Minnie and Sarah (inside car). As Santa Maria expanded after WWI, many "corner" or "neighborhood" groceries were built for customer Convenience. (Photo courtesy Bob De Armond)

Above: Mill St. & Miller St. Corner Grocery.

Right: Purity Grocery —a "modern" chain store. Razed for redevolpment. (Photo courtesy Bob De Armond)

Bill Kraft's Grocery — 601 S. Thornburg — built 1924. Later bought by Chuck Felmlee, when Bill moved to Lincoln & Orange Grocery.

Corner Grocery — Lemon & Thornburg Sts.

Typical grocery check out counter, circa 1950. *L-R:* Electric cash register, charge ticket book, string and wrapping paper, meat scales, grocery scales, hand calculator w/tape. Persons not identified. (Moore/Coleman Photo)

Above: "Little Store" — 500 E. Boone Corner Grocery.

Right: Sisquoc Store and Tanglewood Market.

LOCAL BANKING & FINANCE

Los Angeles First National Bank, later Security First National Bank. On NW cor. Broadway and Main St. (Photo Courtesy Floyd Snyder)

First National Bank of Santa Maria. Later Bank of Italy and Bank of America. On NE cor. Broadway and Church St. During parade. (Moore/Coleman photo)

Security First National Bank, formerly Santa Maria Savings and Loan. NE cor. Lincoln and Cypress streets. (Photo by Stonehart Studio. Courtesy SM Chamber of Commerce)

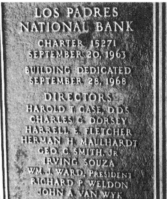

Above: Orcutt Post Office, then Orcutt Branch Midstate Bank. (Photo 1995)

Right: Dedication plaque of Los Padres National Bank.

Hacienda National Bank — estab. 1988. Offices 361 Town Center West. Redevelopment replaced old houses on 100 blk. W. Cook St.

Los Padres national Bank building. Bought out by Wells Fargo in 1972. NE cor. Main & Miller streets on site of old Main St. School.

Hacienda National Bank Directors — 1995. *L to R Front:* Louis Baker, Cheryle Mangino-Diaz, Burt Fugate, Bill Tandy. *Rear:* Hans Kardel, Dick Hulme, Joe Olivera (chmn), Dean Viker. (Photo @ Quality Photo — Courtesy Joe Olivera)

Bank of Santa Maria — estab. 1978. 528 So. Broadway Branch.

Bank of Santa Maria Directors — 1991. *Standing L to R:* Joseph F. Ziemba, Joseph Sesto Jr., William L. Snelling, Wm. A. Hares (chmn-CEO), Richard E. Adam, Roger A, Ikola, A.J. Diani (chmn.) *Seated:* Fred L. Crandall, Jr., Mitsuo Taniguchi, Armand Acosta, Toshiharu Nishino. (Photo from bank report)

Santa Maria Financial Center — 2200 blk. So. Broadway. Built 1981-88 by R.H. Tesene.

EARLY INDUSTRY

Above: Roemer & Roemer 100 blk. E. Mill St. manufactured farm machinery. They designed and patented this beet cutter. Circa 1916. (Photo courtesy Glenn Roemer)

Below: Roemers also built high school bus bodies — circa 1920. (Photo courtesy Glenn Roemer)

Above: Froom Tanks stored water for homes & ranches all over the central coast. (Photo courtesy Bob & Nancy De Armond)

Below: Santa Maria Laundry — W. Main St. (Photo courtesy Bob & Nancy De Armond)

Right: Sanitary Laundry — *L to R:* Zora Sanford (dressed for rodeo), Clyde Johnson. Circa 1940. (Photo courtesy Amber F. Castillo.)

Left: Novo Blacksmiths at work. At left Maurice Novo. At right Angelo Novo Sr. (Photo courtesy Albert Novo)

Above: Imperial Ice cooled ice boxes and freight cars since 1905. (Photo courtesy Bob & Nancy De Amond.

Left: G. Iliff & Son mining sand w/shovel near SM River during WWII. (Photo courtesy Dale Iliff)

INDUSTRY

Natural gas storage tanks — were on RR Ave. (Photo courtesy Owen Rice)

Union Sugar Factory — Betteravia. First major industry in valley — closed 1994. (Photo courtesy Tommy Rice)

Left: Cat Canyon oil fields — one of many on which local oil industry based. (Photo courtesy Tommy Rice)

Below: Steam engines powered most heavy transport for nearly 100 years. (Photo courtesy Tommy Rice)

Main transformer station— S. Depot St.

Above: Coca Cola plant — cor. Jones & McClelland St. Built in early 1930's on site of miniature golf course closed by depression.

Below: Diablo Canyon Nuclear Plant No. of Avila Beach.

Vineyards have replaced beanfields. Wine production is now a major industry in SM Valley area. (*SM Times* photo)

1959 Vandenberg AFB missile launching. Policy shifts in the 1990's include commercial space launches. (Photo courtesy Ken Park)

OIL WELLS & DERRICKS

Shell Beach Oilfields (now Sunset Cliffs housing and Spyglass Inn sites) — Union Oil Co. of California, LaGraciosa and Associated Oil's pump station. (Photo courtesy Jeanett Sainz)

Santa Maria Valley oil fields — view E. on Pertussi Lease — near Betteravia and Blosser roads in 1950's. (Photo courtesy Jeanette Sainz)

Last wooden oil derrick in valley (of many hundreds) — view N. from Orcutt Hill, April 1956, on Rice Ranch Oil Co. Lease. *left:* Roy "Judd" Munger waving Cap.

Photos R. to L: STANDING, GOING,, GONE!

OIL WELLS & REFINERIES

Above: Truck-mounted drilling rigs replaced steel derricks, the forest of derricks in the valley gradually disappeared and pumps & "christmas trees" like this marked oil well-heads.

Below: Off-shore drilling platforms like this opened undersea oil fields off our coast as the onshore fields production tapered off during the 1980's & 90's.

Steel derricks replaced wood for new wells in the thirties. Heaters used to liquefy the heavy crude for ease in pumping and transport.

Part of Conoco Refinery along SMVRR tracks No. of Betteravia. Closed 1994. Now operated by Santa Maria Refining Co.

Unocal's massive Battles "refinery", separator, storage & pumping plant SE of town. Decommissioned and dismantling began in 1995.

Area ranchers and cowboys, rodeo calves near Los Alamos. (Gathering, seperating, roping, branding, vaccinating, ear-marking, dehorning & castrating.) *L to R:* Unknown, Guadalupe Mendoza on black horse w/headed calf, Unknown, Frank Tognazzi, Bill Luton, Dante Tognazzi, Unknown (branding), Harry Confaglia, Al Monighetti, Dante Tognazzi (walking), Manuel Luis (hands on hips), Johnny Bastenchur, Charlie Tognazzi on Pinto w/heeled calf. (Photo by Jeanett Sainz)

HARVESTING CROPS

W.C. Oakley's "modern" stationary grain & bean threshing machine at work — circa 1900. Steam engine burned straw for fuel. Spark arrester screen on top.

Mobile combined harvester circa 1920 pulled by 17 mules and a white horse.

Tractor replaced horses for Owen Rice's bean harvester in 1970's & 80's. (Photo courtesy James O. Rice)

Interior corner of Santa Fe Cannery after disastrous fire — 1954. (Photo courtesy Dawn Karokawa Kamiya)

Sign on bean field — circa 1950. (Photo courtesy Dawn Kurokawa Kamiya)

Harvesting green beans was an all hand labor job in 1950's. (Photo courtesy Dawn Kurokawa Kamiya)

CATTLE RAISING AROUND OUR VALLEY

Cattle grazing on flood plain north of town in early Spring. (circa 1950) (Moore/Coleman Photo)

Cattle still graze valley hills, fattening for market and reducing fire danger. (Photo courtesy Kenneth Park)

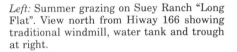

Above: Baled hay replaced hay wagons and hayrides by the mid-1900's. Little hay is produced in SM Valley as machinery has replaced horses, dairies have closed down and irrigated vegetable, grape and strawberry crops have proved more profitable. (*SM Times* Photo)

Left: Summer grazing on Suey Ranch "Long Flat". View north from Hiway 166 showing traditional windmill, water tank and trough at right.

Clarence Minetti and friends retrieving rope while preparing calf for branding. (*SM Times* Photo)

Williams Feedyard. An important facility for cattlemen but a source of noxious odors and angry controversy with residents in nearby NW Santa Maria.

BETTERAVIA'S FRAGRANT FEEDYARDS

Trolley distributing beet pulp along one of many lines of feeding pens at the Sinton and Brown Feedlot. Although many Santa Marians never saw these feedyards, no one could escape the powerful odors that blew thru Santa Maria from the 1930's to the 1980's when the feedlot closed down. "Fifty Fragrant Years". (Photo courtesy Vennie Lee Brown)

Aerial view SE of huge Sinton & Brown Feedyards in 1950. Town of Betteravia upper right. Lines of SMVRR oil tank cars and sugar beet cars in foreground. Trolley line thruout. (Photo Courtesy Vennie Lee Brown)

SUGAR FACTORY & BETTERAVIA

Betteravia Lake — View So. across lake — 1994.

Union Sugar Factory, built 1898-99, Betteravia. Circa 1925. (Photo courtesy Maurice Twitchell)

Betteravia Lake — View west — 1994.

Betteravia residential street — circa 1940. Houses were removed and "Company Town" wiped out in 1968. (Photo courtesy Maurice Twitchell)

Sugar Factory (behind sugar silos) circa 1990 shortly before closure in 1993.

SOME OF THE MANY OTHER SM VALLEY CROPS

Above: Santa Maria Chili barrels. Owen Rice developed and expanded local chili growing, processing and distribution into a major industry of national stature. Eventually the Santa Maria Sailboat brand was distributed over much of the world. (Photo courtesy Owen Rice)

Upper Right: Tomato pickers in publicity photo. Immigrant "stoop labor" did most work on vegetable crops. (Photo courtesy Maurice Twitchell)

Right: Tomato packing shed operation circa 1940. Workers mostly Japanese-Americans. (Photo courtesy Maurice Twitchell)

Green Pea picking. (Photo courtesy Kenneth Park)

Waller-Franklin Seed Farm facilities in Guadalupe. World famous flower seed producer since early 1920's. Now "Waller Seed Farm".

R.C. Wylie's Fairlawn Nursery — estab. around 1910 on So. Railroad Avenue. (Photo courtesy Owen Rice)

Plantel's Scott Nicholson with box of seedlings for transplant, at Nipomo Mesa facility — 1990. (*SM Times* photo)

SANTA MARIA POTATO FARMING — STILL GOING STRONG

Mechanical potato diggers pulled by Farmall tractors. (Photo courtesy Owen Rice)

Mechanical elevator loads trucks fast. (Photo courtesy Owen Rice)

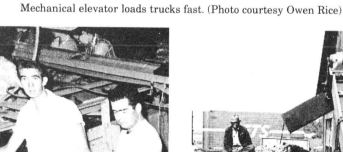

Owen Rice (right) and assistant checking potatos on conveyor belt. (Photo courtesy Owen Rice)

Sacking "Santa Maria Russets" after cleaning, chilling & sizing. (Photo courtesy Owen Rice)

Elevator loading truck. (Photo courtesy Owen Rice)

Potato packing sheds & shipping docks for truck and rail distribution. Cor. So. Depot and W. Morrison streets. (Photo courtesy Owen Rice)

STRAWBERRIES — No. 1 IN SM VALLEY

The 8th annual Santa Maria Valley Strawberry Festival (1994) highlights the importance of the strawberry industry to the local economy. Due to the beautiful Central Coast weather, with mild winters and moderately cool summers the Santa Maria Valley provides an ideal climate for growing strawberries. The local area harvests approximately 6,000 acres of strawberries each year, producing approximately 11 percent of California's berries. (Festival photos courtesy Jana Nichols)

Above: First air shipment of strawberries from SM Valley — 1947. Santa Maria berry farms shipped from Hancock Field. *L to R:* Kenneth T. Sheehy & Robert P. Sheehy. Cooled by dry ice from Union Oil Battles Plant. C-47 military war surplus plane acquired by Flying Tiger Air Freight. Destination Chicago. (Photo courtesy Terry Sheehy)

Below: Hancock Field hangers and ramp are still operational in 1995, but not for planes or shipping strawberries. Commercial businesses, cars and trucks operate here, and the ramp is named Oak St.

Above: Close up of strawberry picking.

Left above: Strawberry weeding and picking is stoop labor intensive. Typical picking crew on a cool, misty morning near town. Machines can't pick strawberries (yet!). (Photo courtesy Floyd Snyder)

Left L to R: Sprinkler pipe, trucks, boxes, pickers and portable toilets. (Photo courtesy Floyd Snyder)

A FEW AGRO-BUSINESS GIANTS

Bonita Packing Directors — 1955. *L-R:* Gerald Mahoney, Andy Hanson, Milo Ferini, Waldo Grisinger. (Photo courtesy Henri Ardantz)

Mechanical loading of lettuce boxes — Betteravia farms early 1980's. (Photo courtesy Henri Ardantz)

Right: Mobile cauliflower harvester-packer produces boxes ready for cooler and market — early 1990's. (Photo courtesy Henri Ardantz)

Below: Bonita Packing Co. 700 blk. S. Blosser Rd. — mid 1970's. (Photo courtesy Henri Ardantz)

Bonita Packing Directors — 1985. *L-R:* Henri Ardantz, Patrick Ferini, Milo Ferini. (Photo courtesy Henri Ardantz)

Traditional cauliflower packing lines — Bonita Packing — mid 1970's. (Photo courtesy Henri Ardantz)

Center of Rosemary Farm — Modern scientific farming and experiments by Capt. G. Allen Hancock started in the 1920's. Chicken houses at center, livestock at right. Road and railroad to town at left in this 1931 photo. (H.W. "Rudy' Truesdale photo, courtesy of Harry Clark)

37

TRUCKS

Gularte Transportation Co. — 8 horse team hauling pink beans 1904.

Gularte cat hauling beans thru downtown Guadalupe — 1917. Frank Gularte on top, Tony Perry standing.

Gularte's 1913 Autocar at SP Railroad overpass hauling oil from Casmalia to Santa Maria.

Gularte 1929 Fageol dump truck loading at Sisquoc Mine. Driver A.E. Bento.

H. Thole Trucking, Ralph May driving hard tire truck circa 1915.

Gularte Sterling tanker and trailer — at Bdwy & Donovrn Rd. 1932.

Gularte pulling sugar beet wagon w/catepiller 45 — 1917

Gularte 1933 Kleiber w/29 ft. Pike trailer — 172 mi. trip to LA. Driver paid $8/trip and $4 for backload — 12 hrs. for round trip. 3 miles/gallon.

Gularte pulling 3 hay wagons 2/45 Holt caterpiller — 1917. *L-R:* Joe Gularte, Frank Gularte.

1934 Sterling flatbed & trailer on Hiway 1. Powered by 150 Waukesha diesel. *L-R:* A. Bagdons, Frank Bento.

TRUCKS & BUSES

Gularte Trans. cattle rig — 1936 — NW cor Broadway and Donovan Rd. *L to R:* Bert Azevedo, Art Pinheiro. (Photo courtesy Frank Gularte)

Bradley Truck Terminal in 1940's — E. Arctic Ave.

Auto Club Highway Patrol service truck — vintage 1930 — 1994 Elks Parade.

Above: Greyhound Bus Terminal. 300 blk. No. Bdwy for over 50 years.

Below: SMAT city busses at Mall bus stop. E. Cook St. — 1995.

Above Left: Geo. C. Smith, Jr. "repairing" one of his Dad's new Mack trucks — 1948. (Moore/Coleman photo)

Left: Bowers & Stokes tow truck — circa 1940. (Moore/Coleman Photo)

Below Left: W.B. Johnson tow truck — circa 1940. (Moore/Coleman Photo)

Below: Latest model (1995) truck-trailer rig. *L-R:* Tony Cochiolo, Anthony Cochiolo. Trucking since 1969.

PCRR & SMRR

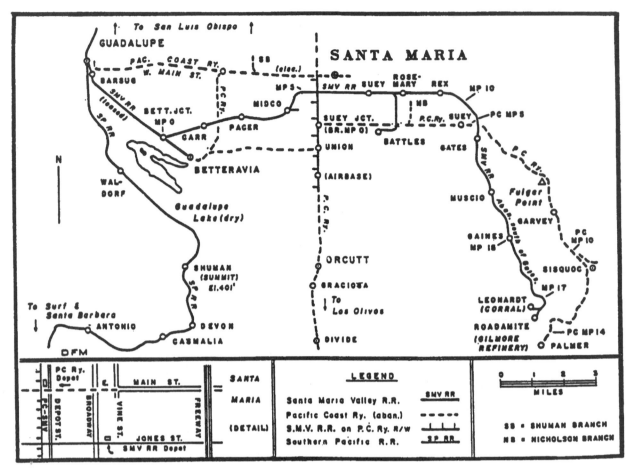

Map of Santa Maria Valley Railroad lines. (Pre - WWII)

PCRR station at W. Main and Depot Streets. (Photo courtesy Tommy Rice)

PCRR train at Los Olivos Station.

Depot Square — a new market. 1995

PCRR electric engine and trolley from SM to Guadalupe circa 1925. (Photo courtesy of Jeanett Sainz)

SANTA MARIA VALLEY RAILROAD (SMV RR)

Steam locomotive fleet at Depot on E. Jones St. circa 1960.

Steam & diesel locomotives share the "roundhouse" repair shop. (Photo courtesy SMVRR)

Diesel locomotive fleet that replaced steam fleet. (Photo courtesy SMVRR)

Icing fresh vegetable refrigerator cars at La Brea Ice Plant facilities. A daily occurrence for over 50 years. (Photo courtesy SMVRR)

RAILROADS AND SMVRR TROLLEY

Original SMVRR freight depot at McClelland & Jones Sts. Built circa 1912. (SMVRR photo)

Attilio De Gasperis in front of trolley in Guadalupe — circa 1925. (Photo courtesy Mr. Degasperis)

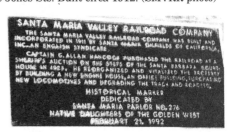

Sue J. Sword, President and Genl. Mgr. of SM Valley R.R. Company since 1969. (SMVRR Photo)

View toward Santa Maria on Guadalupe Road. Trolley track and overhead electric cable on right.

Historic marker in front of RR office honoring G. Allan Hancock's purchase of SMVR in 1925.

SMVRR office staff in front of office. *L-R Back Row:* William Tesene, Mike Parry. *2nd Row:* Betty Sudlow, Jean Farrell, Cardle Rich. *Front Row:* David Jennings, Ruby Brannum, Sue J. Sword. Historic marker at right. (SMVRR photo)

Lathe in SMVRR shop. *L-R:* Cal McDonald, Thomas McDade, Manuel Silva, Gilbert Brown. (SMVRR photo)

Last of original wooden "Railroad crossing, look out for the cars" sign at corner of Jones & Pine.

THE FIRST FLYING MACHINES IN SM VALLEY

Above Left: First airplane to land in SM Valley — circa 1919. Landed on Enos Ranch stubblefield near cor. of S. Bdwy. & Stowell Rd. (Photo courtesy Mrs. Jo Ann Kauffman)

Above: Pilots of 1st plane — Mssrs. Pickup & Thomas in typical pilots uniform of the era. (Photo courtesy Mrs. Jo Ann Kauffman)

Left: First plane crash in SM Valley — circa 1921 at Enos Ranch near Bdwy. & Stowell Rd. Corner. (Photo courtesy Mrs. Jo Ann Kauffman)

Left: May Bros. (Frank & Fred) Service Station at Bdwy. & Stowell.. A convenient source for flyers' gas, oil, tire repairs & rest rooms. Bianchis Market was across the street. Barnstormers sold flights over Santa Maria for $5 — a head — in mid-1920's.

Below: The Richfield Oil Co. Beacon, erected 1927 a mile So. of town, was the first pilot aid in area, featuring a flashing beacon light at night, blue neon lettering "Richfield" on 2 sides, and the initials SM on the third side. Dismantled in 1971. (Photo courtesy David L. Cole)

HANCOCK FIELD OPENS — SANTA MARIA'S FIRST REAL AIRPORT

Top: Grand opening and dedication of Hancock Field — Oct. 21, 1928. Santa Maria's first airport. (Photo courtesy SMV Railroad)

Above: Hangars and flight line — early 1930's. (Photo courtesy SMV Railroad)

Left: Hancock Foundation College of Aeronautics Cadets. (Photo courtesy Kathleen Hulme)

Below: Santa Maria Airlines office at Hancock Field — 1929.

LONG/MACHADO AIRFIELD & NORTHSIDE AIRPARK

Bill and Patricia Lotz visiting Machado Airport on Bill's birthday — May 24, 1957. (Photo courtesy Patricia Lotz Galyen)

Long/Machado Airfield during Jan 16, 1952 washout of S.M. River levee. Airport started by Carl Long circa 1945, taken over a year or so later by Tony Machado after Long died in a crash. Operated until around 1958. (Photo courtesy SMVRR)

Tony Machado.
(Photo courtesy Edna Andreas)

Tony Machado towing plane in Elks Parade in 1950's.

Northside Airpark 1988. Started as small field w/2000 ft. runway for flying lessons, Airpark now limited to helicopters for crop dusting. (Photo courtesy Bob Ross)

Crop dusting by war surplus bi-plane in 1950's. (Moore/Coleman photo)

Crop dusting by helicopter — circa 1990. (*SM Times* photo)

SM ARMY AIRPORT CONVERTS TO SM PUBLIC AIRPORT

Headquarters Santa Maria U.S. Army Airbase built during WWII on 3,069 acres. SM Country Club golf course at rear.

Airbase warehouses & shops along SMVRR spur built to service base. Golf course at rear.

Above: Santa Maria Public Airport terminal, hangar and north end of base (now industrial park & executive golf course) circa 1950.

Left: Public airport terminal — passenger services at left. Wayne Warners crop duster fleet in foreground — early 1950's.

Left: New public airport terminal building. Swift Aire scheduled passenger plane in foreground — circa 1975.

SANTA MARIA PUBLIC AIRPORT

Board Presidents

1962	Wyatt McBride
1963-68	Don M. Prentice
1968-71	James S. Klucker
1971-74	Willis Perry
1975-78	Philip Cardin
1978-81	Willis Perry
1981-82	Christine Castellanos
1983,89,91	Elaine A. Hale
1985,87,89	Burt E. Fugate
1986-92	Richard A Hulme
1988	J. Wesley Kemp
1990,93	Theodore J. Eckert
1994	Muril Clift
1995	Theodore J. Eckert

Airport Managers

1962-65	James F. Brians
1966-68	Arthur E. Johnson
1968-83	Everett W. Berry
1985-94	Dan J. Hoback
1994-96	Brent S. Shiner

District Legal Counsel

1962-64	Robert C. Casey
1964-67	Thomas A. Lang
1965-85	James Rozek
1985-89	Jeffry G. Jorgenson
1989	Anne M. Russell

Above: Airport directors meeting in boardroom — 1986. *L-R:* Bert Fugate, Elaine Hale, Dick Hulme, Susan Mann, Wes Kemp. (Photo courtesy Wes Kemp)

Below: Airport staff — 1985. *L-R:* Brent Shiner, Ruth Libby, Kathleen Kline, JoAnn Berr, Dorothy Hamilton, Dan Hoback (Genl. Mgr.), Jeff Jorgensen. (Photo courtesy Wes Kemp)

Passenger terminal. (Recently named G. Allan Hancock Field) (Photo courtesy Floyd Snyder)

Above: General Aviation Terminal
Below: T-Hangar rentals (SM Public Airport Photo)

James Brians

Dick Hulme

Elaine Hale

Ted Eckert

Muril Clift

J. Wesley Kemp

Brent Shiner

Ken Bruce
Director 1991-95

Ed Hennon
Director 1991-95

Airplane ramp. Hilton Hotel (SM Public Airport photo)

47

SANTA MARIA MUSEUM OF FLIGHT — GOLDEN STATE AIR FAIR

SM Air Museum, Inc. First board of directors — 1984. *L-R top row:* Floyd Snyder, Ron Nanning, H.A. "Bud" Schenk, Larry Fischer, Jim Lucas, Jim Ranger,. *Bottom row:* Milton Barnette, Nancy Morley, Bill Perry (Pres.), Winfield Arata (V. Pres.), Bob Seavers. *Not in photo:* Stan Levy, Jerry Du Rivage, Carl Bowers. (Photo courtesy Floyd Snyder)

First Museum Hangar. (Photo courtesy Katherine Hulme)

Museum's second hangar — donated, relocated and rebuilt after service in movie at SM Airfield. (Photo courtesy Kathleen Hulme)

P-38 and museum interior. (Photo courtesy Katherine Hulme)

Right: Golden State Airfair — line of chalets along flight line and midway — 1993. (Photo courtesy Floyd Snyder)

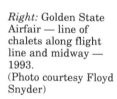

Katherine Hulme
Museum Curator &
Genl. Mgr.

Left: Airfair 1989 Bd. of Trustees.
Top L-R: Muril Clift, Herb Gerfen, Jeanna Yeager, Jim Barach, Diane Cutler, Brent Shiner, Dave Brown, John Beigel.
Bottom L-R: Eloy Renfrow, Dottie Lyon, Mark Witsoe, Jo Wafer, Steve Moeller, Tom Lyon. (Photo courtesy Dottie Lyon)

Right: WWII Army Air Force trainer. (Photo courtesy Floyd Snyder)

Air show formation flying. (Photo courtesy Floyd Snyder)

CITY OF SANTA MARIA MAYORS

Alvin W. Cox
1905-1912

William C. Oakley
1912-1916, 1918-1920

A.F. Fugler
1916-1918, 1924-1932

E.D. Rubel
1920-1924

Marion B. Rice
1932-1946

Alfred Roemer
1946-1948

Alfred E. Gracia
1948-1950

Glenn E. Seaman
1950-1954

Leonard S. Petersen
1954-1956

Curtis Tunnell
1956-1960

C. Clayton "Casey" Kyle
1960-1964

V.L. "Vince" Pollard
1964-1966

George S. Hobbs, Jr
1966-1974, 1980-1994

Elwin E. Mussell
1974-1980

Roger "Rocky" Bunch
1994-

Santa Maria has enjoyed 15 able mayors since incorporation in 1905.

Most of the photographs on this page were copied from the official photographs on display outside the council chambers at city hall.

CITY HALLS — 1905 - 1996

The City Council — termed "Board of Trustees", first met September, 1905 in the directors room of the First Natl. Bank of Santa Maria, NW cor of Lincoln & Main St. The building later housed gas co. offices. (Photo courtesy Tommy Rice)

City Hall 1907-09 was in the Odd Fellows Hall, upstairs in the Haslam Bldg. (Photo courtesy Kenneth Parks)

Third City Hall 1909-16 in City Carnegie Library council meeting room.

Fourth City Hall — 1916-34 at 116 So. Bdwy next to Gardner-Wheaton Drug Store, in front. *L-R:* Harry Krelle, Harry Neel (city engr.), Jack Dennis. (Photo courtesy Barbara K. Nelson)

City Hall interior — 1916-34. Known as the "City Clerks Office" but police, engineer, finance & council chambers all based here. *L-R:* Mrs. Rell Laughlin - secty., A.H. Drexler - clerk, Harry Neel, city engr. Rell Laughlin,- city clerk. (*SM Times* photo)

New (1934) City Hall (first city-owned municipal offices). View from NE on Cook St. in 1941. (Photo courtesy Bob & Nancy De Armond)

Public business entrance to City Hall.

City Council session. Circa 1982.

SANTA MARIA CITY COUNCILS

Santa Maria City Council first meeting in new city hall, 110 E. Cook St., Oct. 1, 1934. *L-R:* PRESS: Mrs. Emma Brians (*Santa Barbara Daily News*), Elwyn Mussell (*Free Advertiser*), Dick Reynolds (*Santa Maria Times*). CITY COUNCILMEN: Alfred S. Roemer, Charles T. Bates, Marion B. Rice (Mayor), Merle M. Willits, Albert A. Dudley. CITY STAFF: Flora A. Rivers, Clerk;, York Peterson, Engineer: W. Bryant Hollingshead, Police Chief; Hurley T. Bailey, Attorney. (Kaiser Photo courtesy of Gordon Gill)

Santa Maria City Council

1905-06	Emmett T. Bryant	1948-52	B.R. Griffith
1905-10	Samuel Fleischer	1948-50	Alfred E Gracia
1905-12	Rueben Hart	1950-56	Leonard S. "Red" Petersen
1905-12	William Mead	1950-62	Curtis Tunnell
1905-12	Alvin W. Cox	1952-53	Allen T. Fesler
1906-08	William C. Oakley	1952-60	James D. MacDonald
1908-12	R.J. Stephenson	1952	Charles T. Bates
1910-14	George Black	1953	Andrew B. Hanson
1912-20	William C. Oakley	1954-60	Ernest T. Sanders
1912-20	A.F. Fugler	1954-58	Vincent L. Pollard
1912-20	C.W. Smith	1956-64	Casey Kyle
1912-18	Ernest H. Gibson	1958-62	Carl W. Engel
1914-18	George Trott	1960-94	George S. Hobbs, Jr.
1918-22	Arthur H. Froom	1960-69	Vincent L. Pollard
1918-22	M.M. Purkiss	1962-65	Charles G. Dorsey
1920-24	Harry Parnell	1962-64	Ed Zuchelli
1920-24	E.D. Rubel	1964-66	David D. Miner
1920-22	E.T. Ketcham	1964-66	Mathew J. Nolan
1922-26	A.F. Black	1965-66	Alfred E. Gracia
1922-26	Fred L. May	1966-67	Gordon V. Dunn
1922-24	Frank L. Roemer	1966-80	Elwin E. Mussell
1924	A.F. Fugler	1966-76	Dan A. Firth
1924-32	C.W. Smith	1966-68	Thomas P. Weldon
1924-28	Ernest H. Gibson	1967-70	Harvey L. Allen
1926-30	Frank L. Roemer	1968-72	Ed Zuchelli
1926-30	J.F. Bradley	1969-74	Casey Kyle
1928-32	Walter W. Stokes	1972-76	Thomas B. Urbanske
1930-34	Sadie West	1974-78	Wayne T. Hesselbarth
1930-46	Marion Rice	1976-86	John "Jack" Adam
1932-33	J.H. Chapman	1976-82	Allen Burke
1932-48	Alfred F. Roemer	1978-82	Toru Miyoshi
1932-40	Charles T. Bates	1980-84	Donald J. Shaw, Jr.
1933-40	Merle M. Willits	1982-84	Robert R. Cutler
1934-38	Albert A. Dudley	1982-94	Curtis J. Tunnell
1938-47	Lloyd M. Clemons	1984-88	James A. "Jim" May
1940-42	Leon J. Libeu	1984-94	Thomas B. Urbanske
1940-44	Kenneth Trefts	1986-	Robert "Bob" Orach
1942-48	Merle M. Willits	1988-92	Dan A. Firth
1944-48	Leonard S. "Red" Petersen	1992-	Toru Miyoshi
1946-54	Glenn Seaman	1994-	Josph "Joe" Centeno
1947-48	Charles T. Bates	1994-	Abel Maldonado
1948-50	E.E. Rubel	1994-	Roger Bunch (Mayor)
1948-52	Vincent L. Pollard		

City Council — 1970. *L-R (Seated):* Ed Zuchelli, Mayor George S. Hobbs, Jr. *(Standing):* Harvey Allen, Dan Firth, Elwin Mussell. (Photo courtesy Chamber of Commerce)

Joe Centeno   *Roger G. Bunch*   *Bob Orach*

Abel Maldonado   Toru Miyoshi

Above: New City Council — 1995

Left: City Council — 1982. *L-R:* Don Shaw, Robert Cutler, George S. Hobbs Jr. (Mayor), Curtis Tunnell, Jack Adam. (Photo by Images)

51

CITY PLANNING COMMISSION

City Planning Commissioners

1929-27	Frank J. McCoy	1956-57	Dr. Arnold Knudsen
1929-33	Asa Froom	1956-60	L.S. Petersen
1929-31	Ed Craig	1956-60	Marion A. Smith
1929-33	Harry Saulsbury	1956-62	Kenneth Trefts
1929-42	Frank Gates	1957-61	Joseph Sesto, Jr.
1929-32	Alfred Roemer	1957-61	Gertrude Chern
1929	York Peterson	1960-62	Douglas Martin
1929	Harry Neel, Jr.	1960-64	Mathew Nolan
1929	J.F. Bradley	1960	Robert Beal
1931-35	R.L. Sandy	1960-66	Elwin Mussell
1932-48	Dr. E.H. Humphry	1960	Robert L. Stuckey
1932-36	York Peterson	1960-77	Joseph A. Olivera
1933-39	Dan F. Donovan	1961-62	Charles G. Dorsey
1933-45	Harry Houghton	1962	Merritt Johnson
1933-36	E. Glenn Seaman	1962	James C. Martin
1936	C.T. Bates	1962-68	Stewart D. Kerr
1936-43	L.C. Donati	1964-66	Malcolm Litzenberg
1936-40	W.A. Vandergrift	1966	Clyde E. Dyer
1939-48	Dr. E.K. Dart	1966-69	Donald A. Reinke
1939-42	Alfred Roemer	1971-75	Robert R. Cutler
1942-43	Leon Libeu	1972-73	James I. Melton
1943-49	C.J. Longwell	1974-76	Jack Spencer
1943	Glen Baxter	1974-79	R.J. Rabska
1943-47	Jack Stanley	1976-81	Curtis J. Tunnell
1945-51	George C. Smith	1976-83	William Couey
1942-52	James D. MacDonald	1976-81	E. Glenn Seaman
1947-54	Ross McCabe	1977-81	Robert P. Diani
1948-56	Blake Cauvet	1979-87	Mrs. Jean Arreguy
1949-52	C.W. Ford	1981-84	Carter Mason
1949-50	Clifford Donati	1981-84	James A. May
1949-50	Lawrence Henry	1981-94	George Paden
1949-54	A.S. George	1984-88	Joyce L. Whiteaker
1950-54	M.N Firfires	1984-88	William C. Byrd
1951-54	Joseph H. Kirk	1985-86	Kenneth Bingaman
1952-55	Paul Sanchez	1986-90	Floyd Snyder
1952	D.A. Darlington	1987-94	Gil Guevara
1952-56	Harry Neel, Jr.	1989-94	Vincent Rodriguez
1954-62	William Fickle	1989-94	James A. May
1954-61	Edward McCoy	1990-	Trent Benedetti
1954-59	Henry LaFranchi	1994-	Larry Lavagnino
1954-58	Mrs. Leo Acquistapace	1994-	Bill Perry
1954-58	Mrs. Albert Missall	1994-	Charles Oberdeck
1956-57	Robert Collins	1994-	Nancy Johnson

Joseph Sesto, Jr.

Douglas Martin

Joseph A. Olivera

Bruce A. McGray

Robert Diani

R.J. Rabska

William Couey

Jean Arreguy

Jim May

George Paden

Floyd Snyder

Gil Guevara

Vincent Rodriguez

Trent Benedetti

Larry Lavagnino

William Perry

Charles Oberdeck

Nancy Johnson

52

CITY SENIOR STAFF

Tim Ness
City Manager

Arthur Montandon
City Attorney

Janet Kalland
City Clerk

Teressa Hull
Treasurer

Dan Shiner
Chief of Police & Fire

William Orndorff
Director of
Community Development

Jack Buchanan
Fire

Alexander Posada
Director of
Recreation & Parks

Michael Cox
Director of Finance

Reece Riddiough
Director of
Public Works

Far left: City Department Heads — 1995.
(SM City Photo)

Above left: Wayne Schwammel — City
Administrator 1984-1994.

Above right: Sandy Boyd - Secty. to City
Administrator , Mayor and Council.

City Clerk (1988--) Janet Kalland, holding
City seal, and staff, *L-R:* Fern Shipley, Gwen
Blackwell (Depty. City Clerk).

Above: "Grogan's Rogues" — City Dept. Head's
informal retirement ceremony May 1989 for
retirement of Bob Grogan.
L-R: Janet Kalland, Mike Maramonte, Jack
Buchanan, Bill Orndorff, Wayne Schwammel,
Russ Matthews, Art Montandon, Bob Hossli,
Reece Riddiough, C. Wright Crakes. (Photo by
Greg Villegas Photography)

City Clerk
Mary O'Brien—
1984-1988.

City Admin. Robert "Bob" Grogan, (1963-
1987) City Clerk Dorothy Lyman, Mayor
George Hobbs. (City of SM photo)

City Staff Awards — 1981. *L-R:* Reece Riddiough, Chester Langenbeck, Edelbert Yeager, La Vonne McGee, Mrs. Charles Coppess, Emma Anderson,
Julaine Snyder, Charles Coppess, Joe Centeno, Henry Pantoja, Mike Farrell, Alice Trefts, Frank Salazar, Bill Abrams, Paul Harper, Gale Brady,
Marjorie Stoskopf, Bill Ryle, Duke West. (SM City photo)

SANTA MARIA PUBLIC LIBRARIES

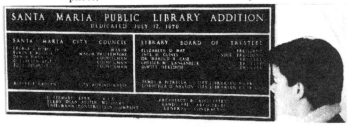

New Childrens wing added 1963.
(SMV Chamber of Commerce photo)

Two story addition opened 1970.
(SMV Chamber of Commerce photo)

Dedication Plaque

Open House dedication speech by library board president Elizabeth Oakley May. Dignitaries *L-R:* Rev. Charle Gibbs, Father Marin, Ed Zuchell, ?, Mayor George S. Hobbs, Jr.

City Carnegie Library — cor. Bdwy. & Cook St. soon after it was built in 1908. Earlier Library was Minerva Club — which donated its collection to the city.

Library circa 1940 — Razed in 1969.
(Moore/Coleman photo)

Jack Buchanan
(*Santa Maria Times* photo)

Dr. Harold Case

Warren D. Kirkwood

The new library — view from Broadway 1940.
(Photo courtesy Marjorie Crawford Martin)

East side of library — 1995

Kirk Higginbotham
(Photo courtesy Bill Nolan)

Frank P. McCaslin
(Photo courtesy Bill Nolan)

Harold English at FBI Shooting
Range (Photo courtesy Bill Nolan)

Richard Long

Santa Maria Police Chiefs

1905-12	G.L. Blosser
1912-16	H.H. Bardin
1916	H.M. Cole
1916	Henry Kortner
1917	A.F. Black
1917-19	J.B. Armstrong
1919	T.S. Lofthouse
1919-21	A.C. Ramsey
1921-26	R.M. Travis
1926-27	J.H. Mahurin
1927	H.L. Neel, Jr.
1927-29	W.T. Feland
1929-30	J.S. Holmes
1930-31	Glenn E. Baker
1931-37	W.B. Hollingshead
1937-40	L.M. McCandless
1940-42	Forbes Barrett
1942-51	W.T. Feland
1943-51	Kirk Higginbotham
1951-56	Frank P. McCaslin
1956-68	Harold English
1968-78	Richard Long
1978-80	William J. Anthony
1980-88	Joseph Centeno
1988-92	Russell R. Mathews
1992-	Dan Shiner

Joe Centeno
(*Santa Maria Times* photo)

Russell R. Mathews

Dan Shiner
(Photo by Doug Coleman)

1920's Uniform

1940's Uniform

Harry Fryer "Motorcycle Cop".
(Photo courtesy Col. Rex Fryer)
Compare Harley's with visiting
Mexican Motorcycle Police. Circa
1926.

Confiscated slot machine to be demolished. *L-R:* Van Diaz, Chief
Harold L. English, Wm. Litzenberg, Wm. Abrams, — Feb 11, 1966.
(Photo courtesy Wm. Litzenberg)

Policeman typing report, circa 1940.

Patrolman Harold English at Police Hq. Radio KSMP in 1940's replaced red light on flagpole for communicating with patrol cars. (Moore/Coleman photo)

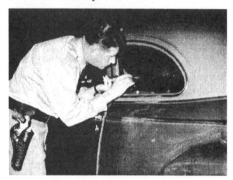

CHP officer dusting car for fingerprints. (Photo courtesy Douglas Coleman)

Chief Richard Long at ceremony. L-R: Officer Joe Centeno, City Councilman Casey Kyle, Mayor George Hobbs, Judge Morris Stephan. Circa 1969. (Photo courtesy Douglas Coleman)

FBI Public Safety Leaders Photography School at Police Dept. L-R Top row: Bud Olson, Frank Crakes, Jim Kelly, Jerry Madson. Bottom row: Lumpoc P.D. rep., Kirk Higginbotham, Arnold Rolland, Gil Stuckey (FBI Agent Instructor) — 1945. (Photo courtesy Bill Nolan)

SM Police Boys Club — sponsors — Eagles Lodge and SM Police. Radio-Phono raffle booth at county fair circa 1947. (Moore/Coleman photo)

Law enforcement officers begin race of mini-gas-operated cars at Chief English's race track in 1963. L-R Front row: Sheriff's Captain Roy Oxford, Sheriff Jim Webster, FBI Agents Ray Millard and Tom Thornton. Back row: CHP Captain Butch Rutherford, FBI Agent Bill Nolan, Frank Corr - D.A. Investigator, Dist. Attorney Vern Thomas. (Photo Courtesy Bill Nolan)

SANTA MARIA'S FINEST

Sr. Police officers at City Hall ceremony. *L-R:* Cmdr. Dave Stern, Deputy Chief Aubrey Patterson, Cmdr. Wm. "Bill" Ryle. (Photo courtesy Doug Coleman)

SM Patrolman Dean Crook with police dog assistant "Jocko" 1989. (*Santa Maria Times* photo)

Sgt. Bob Coleman comforting child evacuated from burning home. (Photo courtesy Doug Coleman)

Left: Sgt. Rad Mawhinney in new patrol car — 1995. (Photo courtesy Doug Coleman

Below: Inspection line up — 1960's. *L-R:* Chief Dick Long, Capt. Lloyd Britell, Asst. Chief Elmer Reynolds, Sgt. Bill Abrams, Sgt. Mike Farrell, Sgt. Don Mize, Sgt. Frank Salazar, Det. Dick Biss, Det. Van Diaz, Motorcycle Officers Steve Voigt, Bill Ryle, unknown Reserve Officer, Paul Lopez, Carl Mosier, Bill Waltizberger, Dan Shiner, Chuck Daly, Les Johnson, unknown Reserve Officer, Pat Gammel Records Clerk.

Police community store front — E. Enos Ave 1995 ribbon cutting by Mayor Roger Bunch. Others *L-R:* Councilman Robert Orach, Coordinator of Volunteers Paul Porpiglia, Cpl. Dee Gunderson, Councilman Abel Maldonado, Police Chief Dan Shiner.

Right: Officer Kendall Greene helpfully pointing the way — 1995. (Photo courtesy Doug Coleman)

Above: Police team taking suspect into custody. *L-R:* Sgt. Bob Reynolds, Jerry Lux. (Photo courtesy Doug Coleman)

Below: Motorcycle officer with radar gun. (*Santa Maria Times* photo)

SANTA MARIA FIRE DEPARTMENT

Right: Circa 1912 — Hose and ladder truck (converted by Crakes Garage) and volunteer firemen. (Photo courtesy Frank Crakes)

Below: 1945 Sunday breakfast, drill and lineup in front of City Hall Fire Station. (Photo courtesy Frank Crakes)

Center: Fire Dept. .vehicles and men on side street circa 1950. (Moore/Coleman photo)

Bottom: 1962 Sunday lineup in front of new fire station at Cook and McClelland corner. (Photo courtesy Frank Crakes)

SANTA MARIA FIRE DEPARTMENT

Santa Maria Fire Chiefs

1900-11 A. McLaughlin
1911-20 Deane Laughlin
1920-56 Frank W. Crakes
1956-71 Harry Bell
1972-94 C Wright Crakes
1994-   Dan Shiner*

*(Police/Fire — combined Dept.)

Right top: Krelle Plumbing Shop fire — 100 blk. W. Main St. around noon brought big crowds of well-dressed churchgoers. Circa 1920. (Photo courtesy Barbara Krelle Nelson)

Right: Firemen stage waterfight for July 4 crowd downtown circa 1925. (Photo courtesy Glenn Roemer)

Above: Historic 19th century hose cart — 1993 Elks parade. *L-R:* John Villegas, Capt. Rick Smith.

Right: Firemen with police support and new foam trailer. Circa 1950. (Moore/ Coleman photo)

Left: Alvin Newton (Photo courtesy Elks Lodge #1538)

IN MEMORY OF WILLIAM ALVIN NEWTON
FATHER, HUSBAND AND FIREFIGHTER
ON APRIL 25, 1970, ON THIS SITE,
FIREFIGHTER NEWTON MADE THE ULTIMATE
SACRIFICE TO THE COMMUNITY,
GIVING HIS LIFE FIGHTING THE BRADLEY HOTEL FIRE.

Right: 1953 city officials hand keys to new dual pumper to Fire Chief Frank W. Crakes. *L-R;* P. York Peterson, City Engineer; Curtis Tunnell, Sr., Fire Commissioner; Glen Seaman, Mayor; Chief Crakes; Russel Griffith, Councilman; Leonard Peterson, Councilman. (Photo courtesy C. Wright Crakes)

SANTA MARIA FIRE DEPARTMENT

Right: Family night dinner at firehouse — circa 1950. (Moore/Coleman photo)

Above: Testing long ladder truck at "Senior Hi-Rise". (Photo courtesy Terry Krelle)

Right: Dousing fire at City Hall — 1952. (Photo courtesy Merv Slawson)

Above: First City Fire Academy— 1975. Firefighter #1 trainees included two women — *L-R:* Denise Perea, Beverly Vaughn. (Photo courtesy Doug Coleman)

Right: City employees of the month — 1995 — SM firefighters — available for photo, *L-R:* Mike Canales, Dennis Szczepanski, Mike Penney, Jim Guerro, Edgar Jansen, James Austin, Mike Champion, Richard Campas, John E. Sabedra.

Above: City volunteer fire fighters quell El Camino School Fire — Nov. 23, 1962. (Photo courtesy Steve Chenoweth)

Apartment house fire — circa 1950. (Moore/Coleman photo)

Trash pile at city dump on E. Main St. Bill Noble in foreground. (*SM Times* photo)

Public Works Dept. Staff laying pipe — 1948. *Back row L-R;* Harold Turner (Street Supt.), York Peterson (City Eng..), John Weldon (Water Supt.), Joe Dilbeck, Harold Rios, Sr., Fred Houk, Albert Leitzke. *Front row:* Arthur Rodriguez, Bill Williams, unidentified, Dave Hayward. (Photo courtesy Tony Galvan)

Trash reduction promotion booth at Home Improvement Exhibition — 1994. *L-R:* Anna Aslanials, "Curby", Lupe Downing.

City Sewer Farm on Black Rd. Christmas tree farm and radio tower at left. (Photo courtesy Tony Galvan)

New mechanical trash can loader & compactor. Billy Brown in foreground. Circa 1987. (*Santa Maria Times* photo)

Above: Scheryn Pratt with rare but always noisy metal trash barrels (superceded by modern plastic containers).

Left: New 90 gal. plastic trash barrels. No more clanging garbage cans. *L-R:* Phil Edwards, Fred May.

SANTA BARBARA COUNTY SUPERVISORS — FIFTH DISTRICT

John Richard Norris
1882-1890

Alvin Cox
1890-1894 & 1898-1902

Walter Elliott
1894-1898 & 1902-1906

William C. "Will
Oakley, 1906-1910

Fremont Twitchell
1910-1915

Leo N. Preisker
1915-1943

T.A. "Cap" Twitchell
1943-1951

Marion A. Smith
1951-1955

Fred Gracia
1955-1963

G. Curtis Tunnell
1963-1975

Harrell Fletcher
1975-1983

Toru Miyoshi
1983-1991

Michael "Mike" Stoker
1991-95: 2nd D. 1990-91

Tom Urbanske
1995-1999

4th District
Supervisors
Representing
Part
of
Santa Maria
Valley

Francis "Mutt" Beatty
1973-1981

Robert Hedland
1981-1985

DeWayne Holmdahl
1985-1989

Diane Owen
1989-1993

Timothy "Tim" Staffel
1993-1997

Some Other Key
Supervisors
(From 1st, 2nd,
and 3rd
Districts)

David Yeager
1977-1989

Gloria Ochoa
1989-1993

Naomi Schwartz
1993-1997

Sam Stanwood
1917-1943

Robert "Bob" Kallman
1975-1990

Tom Rogers
1987-1995

William B. "Bill" Wallace
1977-1997

Willy Chamberlin
1993-1994

Jeanne Graffy
1995-1999

COUNTY OFFICES IN SANTA MARIA

Santa Barbara County Betteravia Government Center Dedicated 1991

Giant mural with historical motif on east side of main Government Center building.

Above: Administrative building including Supervisor's office, hearing room, branch offices of the Assessor Elections, Auditor - Controller, and Treasurer - Tax Collector.

Left: California Condor statue in courtyard of Cook Street and Miller Street County Offices.

SANTA BARBARA COUNTY SHERIFFS

1849-50 J.W. Burroughs	1868-69 N.A. "Nick" Covarrubias	1883-94 R.J. Broughton	1947-62 Jack Ross
1851-52 Valentine Hearne	1870-71 Arza Porter	1895-98 Thomas Hicks	1962-70 Jimmy Webster
1852-54 Charles Fernald	1872-79 N.A. "Nick" Covarrubias	1902-17 Nat Stewart	1970-90 John Carpenter
1854-57 Russell Heath	1880-82 Charles E. Sherman	1918-46 Jim Ross	1990-98 Jim Thomas
1866-67 Arza Porter			

Jack Ross
1946 to 1962

Jimmy Webster
1962 to 1970

John Carpenter
1970 to 1990

Jim Thomas
1990 to Present

Above: 1920's Touring Car.

Right: Lt. Joe Smith . Commander of Orcutt, Santa Maria Valley Detachment 1995

Santa Barbara Country Sheriff's Aero Squadron Deputies at Santa Maria Country Club Sept. 16, 1962. *Front row, L-R:* Sheriff Jim Webster, Tom Allen, Ken Boyce, Gordon Foerschler, Ray Parske, George Miller. *Back rows, L-R:* Ralph Hughes, Jack Crawford, George Burtness, Art Brass, Clarke Paige, Owen Rice, Bob Woods, A.J. Diani, Tony Machado, David Allender, Robert Ross, John Burlingame, W. Swain. (Photo by Roy Oxnard, Captain of Sheriff's Santa Maria Substation.)

Sheriff's Posse Color Guard, Elks Parade, Santa Maria 1993.

1994's Sheriff's all-purpose 4-WD car

SANTA MARIA VALLEY LAW ENFORCEMENT

Santa Maria Valley Constables and Marshals

Constables
Jerry Madsen
Bob Green
Bill Green
1964   Mark Churchill

Marshals
1962-64 Mark Churchill
1964-68 Mark Hite

1968-89 Ronald Rodenberger
1989-92 Robert Casady
1993-94 Tom Gee
1994-   Wes Maroney

County Marshals
1994-   Tom Gee

26,000 copies of "Masters of Deceit" by FBI Director J. Edgar Hoover were obtained by Capt. G. Allen Hancock and distributed widely as a public service. *L-R:* Bill Nolan, Capt. Hancock in Capt. Hancock's office. (Photo courtesy Bill Nolan)

Marshals Staff September. 28, 1988.
Back row L-R: Assistant Marshal Bob Casady, Deputy Garry Martin, Clerk Dolly Slonaker, Clerk Sue Lopez, Deputy Herman Stubblefield, Sgt. Wes Maroney.
Front row: L-R: Deputy Tom Gee, Deputy Jerry Lachance, Marshal Rod Rodenberger. L.S.S. Theresa O'Neil, Deputy Julio Santana. (Photo courtesy Wes Maroney)

Above: FBI Agent Bill Nolan on target range 1963 (one of FBI's best marksmen). He was first Resident Agent in Santa Maria and in charge of office 1944 to 1969. (Photo courtesy Bill Nolan)

Left: Santa Maria Marshal's Staff October 22, 1992. *Back row L-R;* Asst. Marshal Wes Maroney, Deputy Susie Hutchins, Deputy Chris Pappas, Deputy Julio Santana, Senior Deputy Chuck Ward, Deputy Garry Martin, Deputy Ted Rios, Sgt. Jerry Lachance. *Front row L-R:* Clerk Dolly Slonaker, Clerk Sue Lopez, Marshal Bob Casady, Clerk Rosalie Castillo, L.S.S. Britt Stanley. (Photo by Craig A. McNutt. Courtesy Wes Maroney)

Deputy Dist. Attorneys — circa 1993. *L-R:* Ed Bullard, Steve Plumer, Chuck Biely, Jim Craig. (Photo courtesy Chuck Biely)

Retired FBI Agents celebrate Bill Nolan's 75th birthday at SM Inn. *L-R:* Howard Paulsey, Leo Bailey, Dick Jones, Tom Thornton, Bill Nolan. (Photo courtesy Bill Nolan)

CHP "Black & White" patrol car in 1993 Elks Parade.

SUPERIOR COURT JUDGES SERVING SANTA MARIA VALLEY

Samuel E. Crow
1906 to 1932

A.B. Bigler
1931 to 1939

C. Douglas Smith
1940-1941 and 1959-1971

Marion A. Smith
1963 to 1975

Morris J. Stephan
1970 to 1972

Robert E. Trapp
1972 to 1981

Royce R Lewellyn
1975 to 1993

Zel Carter
1981 to Present

Richard St. John
1982 to Present

James B. Jennings
1983 to Present

Rodney S. Melville
1990 to Present

Commissioner Craig A. Smith
1992 to Present

County Superior Court Judges at Santa Maria Courthouse Chambers 1963.
L-R: W. Preston Butcher, Percy Heckendorf, John Westwick, C. Douglas Smith, Marion A. Smith at installation of Judge Marion A. Smith. (Photo courtesy Judge C. Douglas Smith)

SUPERIOR COURTS

C.L. "Leo" Preisker

Plaque dedicating supervisor's room in honor of longtime 5th Dist. Supervisor Leo Preisker.

Retirement for Judge Smith in supervisor's room of Santa Barbara County Courthouse — 1976. *L-R:* Superior Court Judges Charles Stevens, Floyd Dodson, Marion A. Smith, John Westwick, John Rickard, Arden Jensen, Robert Trapp.

Above right: 1954 plaque dedicating county offices (& court) bldgs. 212 E. Cook St.

Right: SM County offices & courtrooms 1964 addition.

Superior Court Chambers in Veterans Memorial Building (wing at far right). Used from 1934 to 1954. (Photo courtesy Laurel Hogle Kelly)

Santa Barbara County Courthouse entrance.

New jury assembly building — 1992.

County offices and courtrooms since 1954. 1992 judicial wing addition at far left.

1992 dedication plaque for new consolidated justice center at Cook & Miller Sts.

SANTA MARIA MUNICIPAL COURT JUDGES

Marion A. Smith
1943 t0 1948

Morris J. Stephen
1953 to 1970

Thomas P. Weldon
1964 to 1969

Richard C. Kirkpatrick
1969 to 1974

Jon Gudmunds
1971 to 1974

Robert G. Eckhoff
1975 to 1985

James B. Jennings
1981 to 1983

Barbara J. Beck
1984 to Present

Michael J. Scott
1985 to 1987

Rodney S. Melville
1987 to 1990

Rogelio R. Flores
Commissioner
1987 to Present

Diana R. Hall
1990 to Present

(Most of the pictures #1 through 12 are copied from the photographs on display at the Municipal Court Chambers in Santa Maris.)

Security First National Bank Building (Former Bank of Santa Maria) Justice Court Chambers 1907 to 1935. On the second floor also Dist. Attorney, Justice of the Peace and Constable's office.

City Hall with Council Chambers at left. Also served as Municipal Court Chambers from 1935 to 1955.

Entrance to Odd Fellows Lodge rooms upstairs for Judge Morris, and his court sessions. (Photo courtesy Kenneth Parks).

Odd Fellows Hall upstairs in W.A. Haslam Building. Justice of Peace — L.J. Morris office & courtroom sessions here.

Bank of Santa Maria (original). Built 1907 — justice court upstairs with entrance off Broadway. (Photo courtesy Mr.s Jean Allen)

Security First National Bank. Courtroom and legal offices continued upstairs in enlarged bank building.

Santa Maria City Hall. Court Sessions in Council Chambers (to left of tower in photo).

North County Branch Courthouse & Office Bldg. — 306 E. Cook St. Dedicated Jan. 1955. (Photo 1995)

ELEMENTARY SCHOOLS

Main St. School — circa 1950.
(Photo courtesy Tommy Rice)

Miller School Courtyard

ElCamino School — 1940's.
(Moore/Coleman photo)

Cook St. School — 1941.
(Photo courtesy Bob & Nancy De Armond)

Fairlawn School (first) — 1930's. (Photo courtesy Bob & Nancy De Armond)

Bonita School (first) pupils on front steps 1927.

Robert A Bruce — SM Elem. School Dist. Supt. 1927-45

Gail Tissier — Supt. SM Bonita School Dist. 1989 —

Bulldozing Main St. School.
(Photo courtesy Richard Chenoweth)

Bonita School (second).

School Board — Santa Maria—Bonita Elementary School District. L-R: Judy Horst, Richard Chenoweth, George Acosta, Mary Burke. Absent - Sue Weiner. (Photo courtesy SM—Bonita Elem. School Dist.)

In 1970's standard earthquake-proof schools like this (Alvin) replaced all earlier schools.

Newlove School in Orcutt Hills near Mr. Solomon.

Ken Milo - Supt. SM Elementary School District 1981-84. 1992 — School Bd.

Jack Garvin - long-time Supt. Orcutt School District. 1979 —

Juan Pacifico Ontiveros School — one of 1990's new schools. Named for early pioneer leaders.

HIGH SCHOOLS

Buses on Broadway loading students from all over the valley including Guadalupe, Betteravia, Bonita, Orcutt, Los Alamos, Garey. Sisquoc, Tepusquet and Cuyama. (Photo courtesy Maurice Twitchell)

School Board — 1938. *L-R;* Walter Stokes, Fred L. May, M.B. O'Brien, Porter Clevenger, Mrs. Gladys Forbes.

Ethel Pope
Dean of Women

"Prof" Wm. J. Wilson
Dean of Men

Andrew P. Hill
Principal

Broadway front of Santa Maria Union High School.
(Photo courtesy Floyd Snyder)

Above: Ethel Pope Auditorium.

Left: SM High School Tower with Golden Cock Weathervane.

Left: Inner court — SMUHS circa 1950.

Below Left: St. Joseph High School Scoreboard

Below: Valley Christian Academy Lion

Righetti High School Steps

71

SANTA MARIA JUNIOR COLLEGE & ALLAN HANCOCK COLLEGE

Original Allan Hancock College Campus — including old Hancock College of Aeronautics buildings & airfield, new buildings and sports field, and newly built College Avenue with saplings. Mid-1950's (Photo courtesy Merv Slawson)

Dr. Gary Edelbrock
AHC President
1977-1993

Dr. Ann Foxworthy
Stevenson — AHC
President since 1993.

Original Santa Maria Junior College building (built 1930's on SM High School campus) reverted to High School when replaced by Hancock College campus. (1995 photo.)

Above: Capt. G. Allan Hancock. Donor of campus & facilities. Named in memory of his only son, Allan Hancock, a victim of the Santa Barbara earthquake. (Photo courtesy SMVRR)

Right: Allan Hancock College Board of Trustees — 1996. *Seated L-R:* Vice President Richard K. Jacoby, President Walt Rosebrock. *Standing L-R:* Robert F. Grogan, Aaron Petersen, Larry Lahr. (Photo courtesy Allan Hancock College)

Business Building — opened 1964.

Below: Historic Hancock College of Aviation offices — later "Airport Hospital", then AHC offices and classrooms. Scheduled for demolition soon.

Humanities Complex — opened 1989.

Consumer & Family Education building — opened 1990.

CHURCHES — OLD AND NEW

Methodist Church (second in Santa Maria)—1892-1921. (Photo courtesy Tommy Rice).

Original St. Marys Catholic Church. 414 E. Church St. (Photo courtesy Floyd Snyder)

Temple Beth El Synagoge. 1501 E. Alvin.

First Presbyterian Church — (1882-1911). Cor. Chapel & Vine St. (Photo courtesy Tommy Rice)

Grace Baptist Church. 121 W. Alvin.

Church of Jesus Christ of Latter Day Saints. 908 E. Sierra Madre.

First Presbyterian Church — (1912-1962). Cor. Cook St. & Lincoln. (Photo courtesy Ida Richards)

Seventh Day Adventist Church. 1775 So. Thornburg. (Photo by Kenneth Park)

The Salvation Army Church (formerly LDS church). 102 S. Miller.

Original Christian Church. Cor. McClelland and Church St.

St. Peters Episcopal Church. 402 S. Lincoln. (Photo by Kenneth Park)

Mt. Zion Church of God in Christ. 419 W. Fesler.

73

CHURCHES

First Christian Church.
1550 So. College Ave

First Assembly of God Church.
3435 Santa Maria Way

New Hope Baptist Church.
416 W. Mill St.

La Luz Del Mundo Church.
520 W. Cypress St. (Photo by Kenneth Park)

Vision of Hope Community Church.
3130 Skyway Dr.

Calvary Chapel of Santa Maria
1265 W. McCoy Lane.

St. John Neumann Catholic Church.
966 W. Orchard.

Four Square Church.
709 No. Curryer

First United Methodist Church
311 So. Broadway

St. Andrews Methodist Church
Bradley Rd. & Larch

Aurora Korean Baptist Church
226W. Dal Porto Lane

Johnson Temple, Church of God in Christ
619 No. Railroad Ave.

CHURCHES

Orcutt Presbyterian Church
993 Patterson Rd.

Bethel Lutheran Church
624 E. Camino Colegio

Calvary Temple Church of God
324 N. Suey Rd.

Church of Jesus Christ of Latter Day Saints
1219 Oak Knolls Rd.

St. Marys of the Assumption Catholic
Church — 414 E. Church St.

First Church of Christ Scientist
841 E. Boone St.

Church of the Nazarene
1026 E. Sierra Madre.

St. Louis de Montfort Catholic Church
1190 E. Clark Ave.

Pine Grove Baptist Church
5551 S. Bradley Rd.

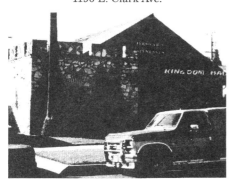

Jehovah's Witnesses — Kingdom Hall
608 W. Church St.

First Baptist Church
2970 Santa Maria Way

Whoever Will Pentecostal Church
500 W. Church St.

CHURCH ACTIVITIES

Baptism of daughter of Alan Kyle and Grace Young Kyle by Rev. Claire Nesmith. (Photo by Vern Houghton.)

Sunday School class led by Otha and Marcelline Eggleston. (Photo by Vern Houghton)

Heifer donated for delivery to West European farmer for self-help recovery from post WWII food shortages. *L-R:* Donor, Hans Melschau, Rev. Oscar Newby, Over 40 delivered. (Photo by Vern Houghton)

Hard Times Party by Methodist Couples Club. Held annually after income tax filing date. *Facing camera L-R:* unknown, Mrs. Troy Hill, Rev. Claire & Gladys Nesmith, Marcelline & Otha Eggleston, Mildred Huddleston, Carl Huddleston with pitcher. (Photo by Vern Houghton)

Services at Cross on the Hill at Methodist Arroyo Grande Camp. (Photo by Vern Houghton)

Wedding of Marian Melschau, daughter of Hans and Lillian Melschau. (Photo by Vern Houghton)

The Minerva Club

The Minerva Club, one of the oldest women's clubs in California, has been a powerful moral, spiritual, cultural, intellectual and social civilizing force in Santa Maria Valley. Founded in a male-dominated society, in 1894, it has quietly exerted a profound influence in improving the quality of life for the community, its families and especially its women and children. The Minerva Club grew from an initial membership of 25 pioneer women to over 500. Among its thousands of beneficial activities over the past century are : Creation of the public library, park improvements, schoolhouse upgrades, sponsoring speakers, musical and theatrical productions, student scholarship luncheons, wartime volunteer work and beautification of the city and valley.

Club auditorium and stage with carved motto "Higher Knowledge and Better Morals" while members engage in traditional Christmas gift-wrapping for under privileged. Circa 1940. (Moore/Coleman photo)

Clubhouse at corner of Boone and Lincoln Streets — built 1928 by Dick Doane for $12,000. Designed by Julias Morgan, renowned architect of Hearst Castle.

Santa Maria Minerva Club Presidents

1889-90	Mrs. Ormonde P. Paulding
1894	Mrs. Leo E. Blochman
1895	Mrs. Wm. T. Lucas
1895	Mrs. Sam B. Slade
1895	Mrs. James F. Goodwin
1896	Mrs. Minerva Thornburg
1896	Mrs. George Smith
1896	Mrs. Harry H. Harris
1896	Mrs. Ormonde P. Paulding
1897	Mrs. Madison Thornburg
1897	Mrs. A.N. Farrington
1897	Mrs. E.S. Fauntleroy
1898	Mrs. Archibald McNeil
1898	Mrs. J. Allott
1899	Mrs. James F. Goodwin
1899	Mrs. Robert Travers
1899	Mrs. Wm. F. Whiteside
1901	Mrs. Ida May Miller
1902	Mrs. Madison Thornburg
1902-03	Mrs. Ida May Miller
1903-04	Mrs. James F. Goodwin
1904-06	Mrs. Theodore R. Finley
1906-08	Mrs. George W. Lincoln
1908-09	Mrs. L.O. Fox
1909-11	Mrs. Wm. C. Adam
1911-12	Mrs. Edward Morris
1912-13	Mrs. J. Mosher
1913-14	Mrs. Charles W. Kitt
1914-15	Mrs. Nelson C. Smith
1915-17	Mrs. J.H. Winters
1917-19	Mrs. John N. Watson (Kate Alida)
1919-20	Mrs. Robert E. Easton (Ethyl)
1920-21	Mrs Earl L. Hazard (Bessie)
1921-22	Mrs. Fred J. Goble (Grace)
1922-23	Mrs. Wilbur L. Hopkins
1923-24	Mrs. Frank H. Gates (Mabel)
1924-26	Mrs. E.T. Ketcham
1926-27	Mrs. Scott F. Sinclair (Bena)
1927-28	Mrs. Major P. Baker
1928-29	Mrs. John H. Youngling
1929-30	Mrs. D.D. Smalley
1930-32	Mrs. Calvin Funk (Grace)
1932-33	Mrs. Jesse H. Chambers (Myrle)
1933-34	Mrs. W. Dale Harkness
1934-35	Mrs. A.P. Catlin
1935-36	Mrs. Ross E. McCabe (Helen)
1936-37	Mrs. Holmes E. Tabb (Bess)
1937-38	Mrs. Charles G. Baird

1938-39	Mrs. Harry C. Dorsey (Ethel May)	1963-64	Mrs. William C. Rice (Lorna)
1939-40	Mrs. A.P. Catlin	1964-65	Mrs. Wm. N. McLellan (Ginny)
1940-41	Mrs. John Stout	1965-66	Miss Elizabeth Scott (Betty)
1941-42	Mrs. Lloyd M. Clemons (Gertrude)	1966-67	Mrs. Asa Hoffman (Janice)
1942-43	Mrs. Ted Baun	1967-68	Mrs. Bert L. Young (Doris)
1943-44	Mrs. W. Leland Smith (Julia)	1968-69	Mrs. Leona Coughlan
1944-45	Mrs. Paul L. Nelson (Dorthea)	1969-70	Mrs. James Hosn (Betty)
1945-46	Mrs. Allen T. Fesler	1970-71	Mrs. Robert J. Sklenicka (Dorothy)
1946-47	Mrs. Errett Allen (Bertha)	1971-72	Mrs. Leonard J. Crabtree (Ruth)
1946-47	Mrs. Leonard S. Petersen (Estella)	1972-73	Mrs. Leo C. Bailey (Bonnie)
1947-48	Mrs. Frederick O. Sherrill, Sr. (Betty)	1973-74	Mrs. Alfred J. Perlman (Rosalind)
1948-49	Mrs. Kenneth E. Trefts (Alice)	1974-75	Mrs. Joseph F. Ziemba (Marjorie)
1949-50	Mrs. Harold T. Case (Lois)	1975-77	Mrs. Joseph A. Lutz (Beverly)
1950-51	Mrs. Jules Bertero (Mary)	1977-78	Mrs. Margaret Diani
1951-52	Mrs. Leo E. Acquistapace (Marian)	1978-79	Mrs. Eugene Ryan (Mary)
1952-53	Mrs. John N. Stewart (Edna)	1979-81	Mrs. Robert J. Klein (Kitty)
1955-56	Mrs. Fred L. May (Beth)	1981-82	Mrs. Clement Gurko (Virginia)
1955-56	Mrs. H. Stanley Brown (Vennie Lee)	1982-83	Mrs. J.P. Lindberg (Laura)
1956-57	Mrs. Burns Rick (Maxine)	1983-84	Mrs. Frederick Gervais (Dobby)
1957-58	Mrs. H. Herbert Law (Cathy)	1984-85	Mrs. W. Newton Price (Jean)
1958-59	Mrs. Ernest E. Righetti (Mildred)	1985-87	Mrs. Robert E. Bonner (Marjorie)
1959-60	Mrs. Dewitt Meredith (Helen)	1987-89	Mrs. Ray Hickman (Betty)
1960-61	Mrs. Henry W. Dixon (Winifred)	1989-91	Mrs. Alan Kyle (Grace)
1961-62	Mrs. E.W. Boyd (Leonora)	1991-92	Mrs. Carl Bryan (Alice)
1962-63	Mrs. Dennis A.C. Dallaston (Virginia)	1992-93	Mrs. Frederick Gervais (Dobby)
		1993-94	Mrs. Grace Kyle
		1994-95	Mrs. Margaret Llewelyn (Maggie)

SANTA MARIA VALLEY CHAMBER OF COMMERCE

CHAMBER OF COMMERCE AWARDS

Robert F. Grogan Award for Public Service:

1990	Robert F. Grogan
1991	Mike Maramonte
1992	Joe Centeno
1993	Robert Hossli
1995	Joe Hagerman

Athena Award

1986	Darlene Watts
1988	Bonnie Royster
1989	Judge Barbara Beck
1990	Diane P. Alleman-Stevens
1991	Peggy Blough
1992	Georgianne Ferini
1993	Anne Fugate

Small Business Person of the Year

1986	George Jeffers
1987	Bill Frainer
1988	Bonnie Royster
1989	Bill Byrd
1990	Bill Perry
1991	Vicki Clift
1992	Kathy Gilliland
1993	Don Lahr, Jr.
1995	Bud Neighbors

Citizen of the Year

1966	Leland J. "Butch" Simas
1966	Dorothy Datter
1967	William Bernhardt
1967	Mae Lapp
1968	Robert L. Nolan
1969	Elwin F. Mussell
1970	Carl W. Engel
1971	Catherine Kanter Carey
1972	Dorothy Lyman
1973	Clarence Minetti
1974	Joe Sesto
1975	George C. Smith
1976	Margie Ziemba
1977	O.P. Chase
1978	Dr. Robert Miller
1979	Sammy Minami
1980	Sue Sword
1981	Rev. J. Stanley Parke
1982	Chuck Hebard
1983	Joe White
1984	Henri Ardantz
1985	Joe Hagerman
1985	Mike Rubcic
1986	Bill Coltrin
1987	Brian Hall
1988	Dottie Lyons
1989	Herb Gerfen
1990	Don Lahr, Sr.
1991	Tony Cossa
1992	Darwin Sainz
1993	Joseph A. Olivera, Jr.
1995	Jay Will

SANTA MARIA VALLEY CHAMBER OF COMMERCE PRESIDENTS

1947	Andy Hanson
1949	Hollis Terry
1950	Gene Brown
1951	Dr. August Mollath
1953	Marion Smith
1954-55	Joe Sesto Jr.
1955	Ed Laubengaylery
1956	Glenn Seaman
1957-58	Worth Coleman
1959	Frank Toller
1960	Charles Dorsey
1961	A.T. Carrington
1962	W.H. McBride
1963	Lorne Carlson
1964	A.J. Diani
1965	W.J. Ward
1966-67	Robert L. Nolan
1967	Martin Paulson
1968	Daniel J. Kirk
1969	Carl W. Engel
1970	James J. Hare
1971	Robert S. Magee
1972	Roger Phillips
1973	Frances Beaver
1974	George Crosby
1975	O.P. Chase
1976	Sue Sword
1977	Dr. Robert Miller
1978	Roy W. Martens
1979	Ben E. Russell
1980	Chuck Hebard
1981	Joe Hagerman
1982	Mike Rubcik
1983	Tony Cossa
1984	Jim Diani
1985	Don Lahr
1986	Jerry Hurley
1987	Alex Hannum
1988	Dr. Betty S. Tibbs
1989	W. II. "Bill" Coltrin
1990	Bill Byrd
1991	Bob Engel
1992	Gordon Gill
1993	Alex Simas
1994	Mike Warren
1995	Bonnie Royster

EXECUTIVE DIRECTORS

Charles Diehle
Jess Chambers
Joe Venable
Bob Seavers
Charlie Jackson
Debbie Timm
Bob Hatch

Carl Engel   Joe Hagerman   Mike Rubcik

Jerry Hurley   Dr. Betty Tibbs   Bill Coltrin

Bonnie Royster   Executive Director Bob Seavers and Staff

Above: Chamber sign on Broadway

Left: El Camino Real bell in front of offices

Right: Board of Directors — 1993. *L-R upper row:* Harrell Fletcher, Dottie Lyon, Jack Garvin, Sylvia Grayham, Bob Engel, Nancy Stewart, Charles Stauffer, Susan Bell, Maggi Daane, Ann Green, Mike Welch, Bonnie Cavanaugh, Hilda Zacarias, Craig Stephans. *Front Row:* Joe Sesto, Karen McConnell, Alex Simas, Ron Myers. (Chamber of Commerce photo)

SANTA MARIA VALLEY ECONOMIC DEVELOPMENT ASSN. "THE DEVELOPERS"

FOUNDERS 1961

Stuart A. Bartleson
Thomas C. Beggs
Mario A. DeBernardi
A.J. Diani
William H. Holman, Jr.
Bjarne Iversen
Jerry W. Justen, M.D.
George O. Radford
James H. Ranger
Burns Rick
Joseph Sesto, Jr.
Merle Wainwright
Wayne E. Warner
Jake L. Will
Edward L. Williams

PRESIDENTS

1961-62	Joseph Sesto Jr.
1963	George D. Radford
1964	James H. Ranger
1965	Robert N. Winters
1966	A.J. Diani
1967	George C. Smith Jr.
1968	Robert S. Magee
1969	Robert L. Nolan
1970	Roger C. Phillips
1971	James I. Melton
1972	Bill C. Perry
1973	Karl E. Wellman
1974-80	Keith V. Lapp
1975	Donald E. Lahr
1976	John A. McGregor
1977	O.P. Chase
1978	Mark J. Smith
1979	Walter Rosebrock
1981	Charles R. Hebard
1982	Alex Hannum
1983	James M. Hagerman
1984-85	Bill Byrd
1986	Raymond Deutsch
1987-88	Herb Gerfen
1989	Tony Cossa
1990	James A Diani
1991	Roger G. Bunch
1992-93	Dottie Lyon
1994	Mike Warren
1995	Carl Engel Jr.

Wm. H. Holman

Jerry W. Justen

George Radford

Jim Ranger

A.J. Diani

Jake Will

Robert L. Nolan

Roger Phillips

Don Lahr

Mark J. Smith

Walt Rosebrock

Chuck Hebard

Alex Hannum

Bill Byrd

Herb Gerfen

Tony Cossa

Robert Royster

Charlie Stauffer
(Board Member)

Jim Diani

Dottie (Renfro) Lyon

Dick Hulme

Jim Weston
(Board Member)

79

SERVICE CLUBS

Santa Maria Rotary Club — April 28, 1936. Among the town's leading "Shakers & Movers". (Photo courtesy Fred O. May)

SANTA MARIA ROTARY CLUB PRESIDENTS

1922-24	Jesse Chambers	1938-39	George Scott	1953-54	Robert W. Poole	1968-69	Walt Gregory	1984-85	Hans J. Kardel
1924-25	Leo Preisker	1939-40	T.A. Twitchell	1954-55	C.W. Ford	1969-70	Dennis Dallaston	1985-86	Keith V. Lapp
1925-26	Art Church	1940-41	Morris J. Stephan	1955-56	Clifford Roemer	1970-71	Jack Gilliland	1986-87	Gerald L. Bartell
1926-27	Lou Crawford	1941-42	B.R. Griffith	1956-57	Charles G. Dorsey	1971-72	John Spencer	1987-88	William Tibbs
1927-28	L. D. Waller	1942-45	Fred Sherrill	1957-58	George C. Smith	1972-73	William J. Ward	1988-89	Leroy Small
1928-29	Frank Gates	1943-44	Clyde Dyer	1958-59	Winston F. Wickenden	1973-74	S. Jon Gudmonds	1989-90	Robert Miller
1929-30	Ross McCabe	1944-45	Joe Robinson	1959-60	Ezra C. Lyon	1974-75	H. Stanley Brown	1990-91	Ben Russell
1930-31	D.T. Batchelder	1945-46	Curtis Tunnell	1960-61	Allen West	1975-76	Charles A. Hebard	1991-92	Robert Acquistapace
1931-32	Harry Dorsey	1946-47	Allen Fesler	1961-62	Galen Hartwich	1976-77	Robert N. Winters	1992-93	Kem Weber
1932-33	Dr. T.H. Conser	1947-48	Edward W. Adler	1962-63	Frank Toller	1977-78	Lane E. Bryant	1993-94	Anthony W. Cossa
1933-34	Walter Stokes	1948-49	Fred L. May	1963-64	William Holman, Jr.	1978-79	Peter K. Weber	1994-95	Peter Donohue
1934-35	W.J. Wilson	1949-50	York Peterson	1964-65	Carl Engel	1979-80	Maurice F. Twitchell	1994-95	Robert J. Schmitt
1935-36	Robert Bruce	1950-51	Ray Hardy	1965-66	Billy Bellis	1981-82	Donald E. Lahr		
1936-37	Dr. August Mollath	1951-52	Everett Sword	1966-67	Robert Magee	1982-83	Frederick O. Sherrill		
1937-38	Herschel Scott	1952-53	Frank Brown	1967-68	Allan Woods	1983-84	Clark Miller		

Above: Kiwanis of Orcutt in front of Santa Maria Public Airport Terminal summer 1995. A very active, fully integrated, community support group. *L-R front row:* Dan Lopez, Debra Peterson, Gail Tissier, Barbara Healy, Elvia Asencio, Richard Siegal, Dennis Neal, Douglas Wilson, Luis Escobar. *Second row:* Jim May, Jim Simpson, Sal Giafaglione, Mary Morton, Stephanie Robb, Mark Buchman, Jim Stroud, Bill Beebe, Ed Robinson, Wes Maroney, Jerry Riezebos, Robert Ostrin, Lawrence Scott, Richard Giachetto, John Higson, David McNeil, Jim Spallino. *Third Row:* Tim Voss. Chuck Biely, Steve Freeman, Maurice Macare, Juvie Rodriguez, Doug Bradley. (Photo by Luis Escobar.)

Rotary Logo Wheel — shown in parade circa 1940. Built by MGM Studio Craftsmen for Cecil B. DeMille who presented it to SM Rotary around 1923. DeMille was a frequent guest of the club during his residence at the SM Inn while he produced the epic film "The Ten Commandments" in the Guadalupe Dunes. (Moore/Coleman photo)

SANTA MARIA VALLEY PIONEER ASSN.

SANTA MARIA PIONEERS ASSN. PRESIDENTS

1924-25 T.W. Twitchell	1951-52 Fred May	1974-75 Ivan "Happy" Worsham
1925-26 W.H. Rice	1952-53 Dave Boyd	
1926-27 W.C. Oakley	1953-54 Barbara Sumner	1975-76 Chester A. Norris
1927-28 W.C. Tunnell	1954-55 James G. Battles	1976-77 Robert Rivers
1928-29 Judge L.J. Morris	1955-56 Ellis Fesler	1977-78 Edward "Crow" James
1929-30 Judge S.E. Crow	1956-57 Monica Bradley Touchstone	
1930-31 M.P. Baker		1978-79 Alex Ontiveros
1931-32 H.R. Saulsbury	1957-58 George Radke	1979-80 Alex Ontiveros
1932-33 H.C. Tunnell	1958-59 Opel Fry	1980-81 Pauline Lownes Novo
1933-34 John Fesler	1959-60 Leslie R. Holland	
1934-35 Alice Lewis	1960-61 Gertrude France	1981-82 Betty McDonald
1935-36 A.F. Black	1961-62 Chester A. Davis	1982-83 Curtis Tunnell
1936-37 Joe S. Calderon	1962-63 Gertrude M. Clemons	1983-84 Parnell Tilley
1937-38 Lou S. Drumm		1984-85 Parnell Tilley
1938-39 Frank C. May	1963-64 Marinus Neilsen	1985-86 Sue Stenner Krafft
1939-40 Jack H. Glines	1964-65 Ida Wylie Jones	1986-87 Vivian Litten Dutton
1940-41 Manuel Bello	1965-66 Morris J. Stephan	1987-88 Clarence Donati
1941-42 Gaylord Jones	1966-67 Elizabeth Oakely May	1988-89 Clarence Donati
1942-43 Dr. Leland Smith		1989-90 Eddie James
1943-44 Leonard Adam	1967-68 William Elliott	1990-91 Earl Burger
1944-45 Walter W. Stokes	1968-69 Glen A. Roemer	1991-92 Jim May
1945-46 Audel Davis	1969-70 J. Dorean Davis	1992-93 Oliver Nelson
1946-47 Raymond Strong	1970-71 Emilio Sutti	1993-94 Betty Haslam Carr
1947-48 Ida Hawkins	1971-72 William Ruiz	1994-95 Jay Openshaw
1948-49 Ernest Righetti	1972-73 Leland "Butch" Simas	1995-96 Richard Chenoweth
1949-50 Catherine Fickert		1996-97 George S. Hobbs
1950-51 Marion Rice	1973-74 Wilfred "Bull" Saunders	

New Pioneer Park under construction 1995. Cor. Foster & Blosser Rds. *L-R* Board members: Richard Chenoweth, Jay Openshaw, Vicki Wilson, Earl Jennings. (Photo courtesy Pauline Novo).

1995-96 Directors. *L-R:* Richard Chenoweth, Jay Openshaw, Betty Carr, Vicki Wilson, Pauline Novo, Jim May, Clarence Donati. Not present: Oliver Nelson, Albert Novo.

100th birthday of Ellen Kortner Tunnell Sept. 21, 1980. Four generations of Tunnells. *L-R top:* Curtis J., G. Curtis, Teresa (Bruce) Brown, George. *Center:* John, Ellen Kortner, Annie. *Bottom:* Mary Tunnell, Katherine Tunnell. (Photo courtesy Curtis Tunnell. Sr.)

Nearing 100th birthday of Myrtle Launders Hobbs 1996. Five generations. *L-R:* Carrie McNamara Schwartz, Rebecca Lynn Schwartz, Myrtle Launders Hobbs, George Hobbs, Cassie Hobbs McNamara

Descendents of early pioneers Antone Perry (1872) & Manuel Olivera (1890). 4th generation Oliveras. *L-R:* Joe, Wilfred, Gene and Elizabeth Marshall.

Pioneer BBQ fundraisers. *L-R:* Albert Novo, Joe Ramirez, Norman Burke, Bill Hadsell

Jim Gamble "Pumpkin City" fundraiser and master mason for Pioneer Park.

Ike Simas — long time Treasurer of Pioneers and manager of Elks Club.

THE YMCA

YMCA Indian Guide Village at Waller Park — circa 1980. (Photo courtesy SMV Chamber of Commerce)

Beach party picnic — early 1990's. (YMCA photo)

YMCA Championship Basketball Team — 1960. *L-R:* Harvey Taylor (advisor), Clifford Deveney, six other team members, Coach Don Allen. (Photo courtesy Vern Houghton)

Aerobic Dance Class at new YMCA gym — early 1990's. (YMCA photo)

Ribbon-cutting at first YMCA building. *L_R:* Mayor Casey Kyle, Jim Ranger — radio KUHL owner-mgr. (Photo by Vern Houghton)

Front of new YMCA building — early 1990's. (YMCA photo)

YMCA float Elks Rodeo Parade — 1980's. (Chamber of Commerce photo).

First YMCA building. 500 blk. So. McClelland St.

YMCA Indian Guide float — Elks Rodeo Parade — 1994.

SANTA MARIA VALLEY BEAUTIFUL — SINCE 1963

Rose Garden Donor Plaque

Ethel May Dorsey Conrad

Rosalind and Alfred Perlman

Joyce Gilbert, Bailey Hudson and Roy Schmidt planting more trees at Adam Park. (Photo courtesy Brian Hall)

President Brian Hall and Marion Long display Tree City USA award. (Photo courtesy Brian Hall)

Audience at Rose Garden Dedication, Central Plaza Park — 1995.

Clean Campus Award flag raising at Casmalia School. (Photo courtesy Brian Hall)

Dan and Peggy Blough receive Commercial Bldg. Beautification Award from President Marjorie Miller — 1995.

Mayor Elwin Mussell, Rosalind Perlman and friends at kickoff of annual SMVB-sponsored city clean-up campaign. Circa 1980. (Photo courtesy Brian Hall)

SANTA BOARD OF REALTORS PRESIDENTS 1926 — 1995

Santa Maria Board of Realtors Office in 1973 at 309 S. Lincoln St. Started in 1926, board was defunct 9 years during depression, 8 years of WWII and aftermath. Grew from 6 to over 400 members.

Fred L. May
1926-29

George C. Smith, Jr.
(Secty) 1926-29

1939   M.M. Purkiss
1948   H.A. Frew
1950   Bert Wharton
1951   Glen A. Peck
1958&62 Mike Koshell
1959   Chrystal Grabil

M.F. Turnage
1949

"Reg" Evans
1952

Russ H. Omberg
1953 & 54

Don H. Taylor
1955

Paul Fox
1956

Henry La Franchi
1957

Morris Henske
1960

Billie Everett
1963

Wayne Mack
1964

Myrna Winter
1966

Frances Beaver
1967

1961   Bill Hand
1965   Clarence B.
          F'loro
1968   Raymond Webb
1969   Nick Gaynos
1985-86 Dan Firth

Robert G. Evje
1970

Donald De Bruyn
1971

Jaye Armstrong
1972

Jack Bevington
1973-74

Peggy Rector
1975-76

Arlie Lancaster
1977

Joyce Whiteaker
1978-79

Butch Reynolds
1980

Marilyn Harbuck
1981

Chuck Washabaugh
1982

Doris Vosburg
1983-84

Kathryn Williams
1987

Jeanie Hayes
1988

Chuck Ayer
1989

David Skinner
1990, 91, 94

Ken Baker
1992-93

Gail Davis
1995

84

SANTA MARIA ELKS LODGE #1538

First Elks Lodge — 200 blk. E. Main St. — photo 1941. (Photo courtesy Bob and Nancy De Armond)

New Elks Lodge on Elks Lane and No. Bradley Rd. (Elks Lodge photo)

Lodge officers — circa 1950. *L-R top row:* Clarence Minetti, Hobie Hamlin, Dan Chern, Art Bauer, Pop Larsen, Bob Bingham, Dick Weldon, Lou Loving , Harry Andrews, Dutch Zayling, Unknown, Jack Gutchel. *Front row:* Butch Simas, John Weldon, Bink Rubel, Doctor O.C. Jones, Carl Engel, Paul Sanchez, John Murray. (Elks Lodge photo)

Lodge officers and new members — 1964. *L-R upper rows:* Butch Simas, -?, Clarence Minetti, -?, -?, Burton Twitchell, -?, Bob Bingham, -?, Harry Andrews, -?, Dan Chern, -?, Art Bauer, -?, Dick Williams, Tony Cossa, -?, Charlie Cossa, Charles Brannon, Dutch Zayling, James Cobb, T.A. Cossa, Jack Gutchell. *Bottom row:* Frank Bjorklund, -?, Irv Rios, John Weldon, Harvey Melman, Bob Torres, -?, Milo Ferini, Dr. Duke Schneider, Lou Loving, Hobie Hamlin. (Elks Lodge photo)

B.P.O.E. ELKS LODGE #1538 — LEADERS EARLY DAYS 1927-1943

OFFICERS &
CANDIDATES -
1971 - 72

1. - Jack Freddi
2. - Dr. Jerome Justin
3. - Maynard Beall
4. - John Weldon
5. - Ken Biely
6. - Ernest Righetti
7. - Bill Ashbrook
8. - Chet Jones

(Source - Elks Lodge)

Louis N. Crawford First
Exalted Ruler 1927 to 1928

O.C. Jones
1928 to 1929

R.H. Bardin
1929 to 1930

W.D. York
1930 to 1931

Gorton J. Miller
1931 to 1932

Ray Stewart
1932-to 1933

Thomas P. Weldon
1933 to 1934

Ed. D. Cochran
1934 to 1935

Leo Schauff
1935 to 1936

T.A. Twitchell
1936 to 1937

Walter G. Meyer
1937 to 1938

Kenneth E. Trefts
1938 to 1939

R.A. Polley
1939 to 1940

John F. Adam, Sr.
1940 to 1941

Albert S. Missall
1941 to 1942

S.F. Larson
1942 to 1943

86

B.P.O.E. ELKS LODGE #1538 — LEADERS 1943-1963

Fred D. Sherrill
1943 to 1944

B. Russ Griffith
1944 to 1945

Elmer Griset
1945 to 1946

J.D. MacDonald
1946 to 1947

Leonard S. Peterson
1947 to 1948

John S. McDonell
1948 to 1949

Glen E. Seaman
1949 to 1950

R.W. Patton
1950 to 1951

Jeffery H. Madsen
1951 to 1952

Paul Sanchez
1952 to 1953

Edward E. Rubel
1953 to 1954

Carl W. Engel
1954 to 1955

William S. Rice
1955 to 1956

Harold L. Twyford
1956 to 1957

Wayne Warner
1957 to 1958

Blake Cauvet
1958 to 1959

John A. Murray
1959 to 1960

Richard P. Weldon
1960 to 1961

Clarence S. Minetti
1961 to 1963

Leland J. Simas
1962 to 1963

B.P.O.E ELKS LODGE #1538 — EXHALTED RULERS 1963-1983

Robert Torres
1963 to 1964

Lewey L. Loving
1964 to 1965

R. Harry Andrews
1965 to 1966

F. Robert Bingham
1966 to 1967

Arthur G. Bauer
1967 to 1968

John P. Gutshall
1968 to 1969

Burton J. Twitchell
1969 to 1970

Jack E. Poole
1970 to 1971

Ernest E. Righetti, II
1971 to 1972

Kenneth S. Biely
1972 to 1973

William S. Ashbrook, Sr.
1973 to 1974

Chester B. Jones
1974 to 1975

Frank W. Davis, Jr.
1975 to 1976

Marvin E. Griffin
1976 to 1977

Donald L. Aris
1977 to 1978

Edwin W. Walker, Sr.
1978 to 1979

Bill M. McDaniel
1979 to 1980

Ben Del Mastro
1980 to 1981

Norm McDonald
1981 to 1982

Fred Campbell, Jr.
1982 to 1983

B.P.O.E ELKS LODGE #1538   EXHALTED RULERS 1983-96

Allen D. Sorenson
1983 to 1984

William "Bill" Sloan
1984 to 1985

Miles Jacklin
1985 to 1986

Vern Claycamp
1986 to 1987

Clint George
1987 to 1988

Chuck Washabaugh
1988 to 1989

John Knapp
1989 to 1990

Larry Bowman
1990 to 1991

Larry Steinkraus
1991 to 1992

William Stanford
1992 to 1993

Malcolm "Mac" Clark
1993 to 1994

Don Seaman
1994-1995

Ashley Fittz
1995 to 1996

OFFICERS — 1995-96

Exalted Ruler . . . . Ashley Fittz
Est. Leading Knight . . . . Ron Reynolds
Est. Loyal Knight . . . . Keith Barks
Est. Lecturing Knight . . . . Barry Stewart
Secretary . . . . Michael Stith
Acting Secretary . . . . Chuck Washabaugh
Treasurer . . . . Bill Bettale
Tiler . . . . Bobbie Maxwell
Esquire . . . . Keith Bugal
Chaplain . . . . Don Moshier
Inner Guard . . . . Gale Weaver
Organist . . . . Annesley Hopkins

TRUSTEES   1995-96

Larry Bowman

Larry Steinkraus   William Stanford
Mac Clark   Don Seaman

Bob Saving
Elk of the Year — 1995

Ted Scott
Historian

Ron Reynolds
Leading Knight — 1995

Keith Barks
Loyal Knight — 1995

Barry Stewart
Lecturing Knight — 1995

89

UNITED WAY

UNITED WAY CAMPAIGN CENTER

	President	Campaign Chair
1959	Galen Hartwich	Richard Carrington
1960	John Adams	William King
1961	Galen Hartwich	Ross Naylor
1962	Galen Hartwich	Lloyd Stone
1963	Ross Naylor	Rev. Charles Gibbs
1964	Lloyd Stone	Emile Genest
1965	Rev. Charles Gibbs	Jack Burrows
1966	Jack Burrows	Thomas Gocking
1967	Jack Burrows	Daniel Kirk
1968	Willis Perry	Thomas Weldon, Jr.
1969	Antonio Del Pesco	Lloyd Stone
1970	Daniel Kirk	Philip Cardin
1971	Philip Cardin	Steven Cugowski
1972	Philip Cardin	Douglas Felchlin
1973	Jim Hare	Allen Burke
1974	Allen Burke	Jim Glines
1975	Karl Wellman	Fred Barrett
1976	Douglas Felchlin	Marjorie A Ziemba
1977	S. Jon Gudmunds	O.P. Chase
1978	S. Jon Gudmunds	Fred Andriano
1979	Marjorie A. Ziemba	Norman Buvick
1980	Ed Guhl	Kenneth Biely
1981	Gil White	David Aquino
1982	Gil White	Emmett Jones
1983	Margaret Sjovoid	Norman Biane
1984	Cole Lucas	MajGen. Jack L. Watkins
1985	John Larson	Darwin Sainz
1986	Bob Orach	Robert Royster
1987	James Newton	Pricilla Toomire
1988	Darwin Sainz	Bob Engel
1989	Mike Warren	Charles Stauffer
1990	Robert Royster	Bob Orach
1991	John Normanly	Mike Gibson
1992	Charles Stauffer	Diane Woodward
1993	Roger Bunch	Mike Kelly
1994	Bob Engel	Committee
1995	Ron Nanning	Mike Sell

United Way Executive Directors

1978-80	Kirk Sapa
1980-85	Frank Healy
1985-93	Robert Bennett
1993-	Diane Woodward

Marge Ziemba
Campaign Chair
1976, Pres. 1979

Darwin Sainz
Campaign Chair
1985, Pres. 1988

John Normanly
Pres. 1991

L-R: Gail White (Pres. 1981 and 1982) presenting gavel to Dr. Meg Sjovold, 1983 pres.

Above: Bob Engel, campaign chair. 1988, pres. 1994 with United Way logo.

Below: Campaign meeting at The Landmark Restaurant — 1985 — historic mural panels on wall. *L-R:* John Larson (pres. 1985), Major Genl. Jack Watkins (campaign chair 1984), Robt. Royster (campaign chair 1986, president 1990)

Ron Nanning
Pres. 1995

Frank Healy
Exec. Dir. 1980-85

Diane Woodward
Exec. Dir. 1993 —

SANTA MARIA VALLEY HISTORICAL ASSN. & MUSEUM

Museum building and sign

PRESIDENTS

1955-57	Mrs. Ethel May Dorsey Conrad
1958	Ed McCoy
1959	Dick Doane
1960	Walter Conrad
1961-62	Gertrude Rice France
1963	Burton Twitchell
1964	Dr. William Houpt
1965	Richard Weldon
1966-67	Gaylord Jones
1968-69	Dorothea Nelson
1970-73	Ted Bianchi
1974	Jim Glines
1975	George S. Hobbs, Jr.
1976-77	Ted Bianchi
1978-79	Ralph Sutton
1980-82	Robert Rivers
1983-84	Philip Ault
1985	Earl Jennings
1986-87	George Hesser
1988-90	Philip Ault
1991	Bobbie Jennings
1992	Delores Luis
1993-94	Nancy Converse
1995	Joseph S. Kasper

MUSEUM CURATORS

1974-83	Brooks "Bud" Ferguson
1983-91	Luann Powell
1991-95	Marilyn Hoback Cronk
1995 —	Richard Chenoweth

CITY HISTORICAL LANDMARKS*

1. Buena Vista Park
2. Santa Maria Flagpole
3. Site of First City-owned Waterworks
4. Residence of Reuben Hart
5. Pacific Coast Railway Depot Site
6. Santa Maria Inn
7. Santa Maria City Hall
8. Four Corners
9. Veterans Memorial Culture Cntr.
10. Site of First Masonic Temple

Bronze Descriptive Plaques on sites.

CITY LANDMARKS COMMITTEE PLACES OF HISTORICAL MERIT

Alvin Newton — Fireman Memorial
Orange Street Kindergarten
Cypress Street Kindergarten
Old St. Mary's Church
Melby's Clock
Ship *Santa Maria* Bas-relief
Coca Cola Building
Civic Theatre Bldg.
Zanetti Home
First Methodist Church
St. Peters Episcopal Church

Part of BBQ Hall of Fame — added to museum 1995 by R.H. Tesene (in photo)

Luann Powell   Richard Chenoweth

Betty Scott   Joe Kasper

HISTORIC SITES DESIGNATED BY NATIVE DAUGHTERS OF THE GOLDEN WEST

Martin Home/Old Santa Maria Club/
                The Landmark
Santa Maria Valley R.R. HQ.
Heritage Walk

HISTORIC SITES DESIGNATED BY DAUGHTERS OF THE AMERICAN REVOLUTION CAPT. HENRY SWEETSER CHAPTER

George C. Smith Sr. Home

HISTORIC SITES DESIGNATED BY MINERVA CLUB

Foxen Canyon (Fremont Route)
Minerva Clubhouse- (Julia Morgan
   Architect, Designated in Nat. Register
   of Historic Places).

Christmas tree and board members. *L-R:* Adrienne Pimentel Tucker, Ruthanne Tompkins. (Photo courtesy Richard Chenoweth

Teddy Bear Exhibit Reception. *L-R:* Maggie Lewellen, Margaret Kaukonen, Judge Royce Lewellen, Mayor Roger Bunch. (Photo courtesy Richard Chenoweth)

BOYS & GIRLS CLUB

Clifford Donati ranch house on 5 acre site he donated Boys Club around 1969. This is location of Boys and Girls Club facilities on N. Railroad Ave.

A few club members say "THANKS" at new clubhouse entrance.

(All photos on this page courtesy Boys & Girls Club)

Watermelon eating contest

"Pool Sharks" at club — early 1990's.

Learning and fun with computers

"Elvis" visits club. *L-R:* Bill Libbon, "Elvis", Steve Wurm.

"Hawaiian" Dancers

Easter egg hunt on club house site —1977.

BOY SCOUTS OF SANTA MARIA VALLEY

Santa Maria Rotary Club Troop No. 1 at the Scouthouse (old Mill St. School) ready for weekend camping trip — 1938.

Troop 73 of First Methodist Church — 1955. *L-R back:* Dwayne Collins, Dale George, Philip Park, Leonard Lenz, Curtis Tunnell. *Front:* Richard Chenoweth, _ Newby. (Photo courtesy Richard Chenoweth)

Above left: Sea Scouts — wartime drill at Vets Memorial— circa 1943. (Moore/Coleman photo)

Above right: Camporee on shore of Lake Cachuma — 1992.

Left: Troop 212 Eagle Award celebration — 1992. Mayor George Hobbs & City Clerk Janet Kalland at rear right. Troop members *L-R rear:* Eric Green, Tom Thompson (Scoutmaster), Mike Thompson, Mark Payne, unid., Kelly Green, unid, Fred May. *Front:* Vincent Specht, unid, Mark Thomson, Steve McDonald, Mike Green, Steve Thompson, Chris Outlaw, Matt Buontiempo.

Below: Cub Scouts race handmade cars in 1995 Pinewood Derby at Mall.

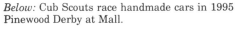

Order of the Arrow Lodge Teepee

Canoeing lessons in Rancho Alegre Scout Camp.

ORCHESTRAS & BANDS

Santa Maria City Orchestra concert at C.V. Gardner residence — circa 1900. (Photo courtesy Gordon Gill

Santa Maria Union High School Orchestra — 1939. *Seated:* Norma Deising, Mary Matsurra, Clay Dennison, Kiyoko Hayashi, Satsuko Ito, Jean Bongard, Claire Peck, Alla Sanders, Patsy McGregor, David Dittman, Donald Corbett, James May, Bob Baker, Georgina Chaffin, Hiroko Araki, Nadine Hickman, Verda Bassi, Alice Chapman, Pauline Lownes, Myrna Jacobson, Doris Anderson, Marjorie Clelland, Ruby Keck, Betty Kortner, Dorothy Whearty. *Standing:* Eleanor Needham, Tom Shutt, Robert Black, Mary Ellen Whitney, Jack Pierce, Lee Jones, Milton Caligari, Lloyd Hamilton, Mary Dena Anderson, Americo Diani, Esther Costa, Albert Novo, Annie Jackson, Winifred Gunther, Sydney Peck (instructor), Jean Chaffin, Judd Chew, Bertha Belle Alexander, Gene Sturgeon, Jim Hapgood, Arthur Pimentel, Clayton Kyle. (Photo courtesy Mary Alice (Martin) Carlson)

Santa Maria Elementary School Band — sponsored by Elks Lodge #1538 at El Camino School. Director Lester Hayes in white uniform at right — 1940's. (Photo courtesy Elks Lodge #1538)

SANTA MARIA SYMPHONY AND OTHER MUSICAL GROUPS

Children's Choir — Methodist Church during 1940's. Bob Huddleston and Patty Boyd at the organ. (Photo courtesy of Vern Houghton)

Santa Maria Symphony and Master Chorale — early 1990's under baton of Patrick Howard Kelly.
(Photo courtesy Santa Maria Symphony Society)

Central City Chordsmen of S.P.E.B.S.Q.S.A. — 1995. (Photo courtesy Gene Kai)

Righetti High School Marimba Band & Ballet Folklorico under director Ricardo Gabaldon.

CENTRAL CITY CHORDSMEN

Glenn Back, bass	Don Gugeler, baritone	Larry Los, lead	Al Schiessl, bass
Jim Berube, lead	Ed Gutierrez, lead	Dick Manning, bass	Louis Schot, bass
Jimmy Berube, lead	Ralph Guthrie, tenor	Dick Mininger, bass	Ottis Scott, tenor
Michael Berube, lead	Mark Hayzlett, tenor	Don Montgomery, lead	C.H. Snitchler, lead
Brad Bormann, lead, director	Gordon Hennies, lead	John Nagy, lead	Warren Sparks, bass
Darrell Boyd, baritone	Luther Hintz, tenor	William Noll, lead	Harvey Taylor, lead
Dan Daniels, baritone	Gene Kai, tenor, assist. director	Makuisa Peapealalo, lead	Dean Ubben, bass
Lloyd Drom, lead	Rock Kirkham, bass	Jack Proper, bass	Paul Van Alstine, bass
John Dykema, baritone	Casey Kyle, bass	Dick Rebenstorf, lead	Reg Wagner, bass
Louis Foltzer, baritone	Bill Leas, bass	Bud Riley, bass	Don Ward, lead
Charles Fredrickson, lead	Larry Long, bass	Paul Ross, baritone	Russ Weed, lead

AHC CONCERT BAND AND SANTA MARIA SYMPHONY

ALLAN HANCOCK COLLEGE CONCERT BAND — 1995
Gary Thompson, Director

Flute
Debra Allen
Ramon Armenta
Torey Graham
Stacie Greenwalt
Laura Johns
Alice McGonigal
Bonnie Ross
Seymour Schwartz

Piccolo
Alice McGonigal

Oboe
Patricia Lynn
Diahanna Wray

Baritone Saxophone
Gordon Hodam
Kevin Laird

Horn
Herb Adams
Dennis Cooper
Deneen Granger
Walt Stier

Trumpet
Matthew Ahola
Cisco Castillo
Robert Gnibus
Robert McGhie
Arnie Monroe
Tim Nunez
Sandy Reynolds
Randall Rust
Forrest Stoll

English Horn
Patricia Lynn

B-Flat Clarinet
David Boisvert
Jeanne Bradbury
Jo Churchill
David Cleveland
Kelly Cooper
Scott Davis
Kris Folkins
Don Gugeler
Lisa Hall
Terry Handy
Dennis Headrick
Chris Hoffmeyer
Valerie Jagoda
Chris Kuzell
Glen Newcomb
Lloyd F. Pipes

Bass Clarinet
Oliver Smith

Bassoon
Lawrence Lee

Alto Saxophone
Dean Aguilar
Carvel Boardman
Lynn Constantino
Bruce Cummings
Jaime Cummings

Tenor Saxophone
Nancy Barlas
Jeremy Spurbeck

Baritone
Larry Appel
Roger Lehman
Douglas Mussell
Dave Rhodes

Trombone
Paul Bascaino
Ron Kane
Tom Lynn
Mark Powell
Leroy Smith

Tuba
Christopher Blomgren
Robert Coburn

Percussion
John Beck
Bruce Boles
Gena Laird
Mary Jane Newcomb
Jason Uva

CONCERT MASTER
Lloyd Pipes

LIBRIAN/SECRETARY
Patricia Lynn

PUBLICITY AND LIAISON
Larry Lee, Nancie Only

UNIFORMS
Dennis Cooper, Walt Stier

Dr. Chris Kuzell — Founder & Director of AHC Concert Band in 1961.

Gary Thompson, Director of Band since 1975.

Santa Maria Symphony Orchestra — Samuel Gorbach conducting at Marian Theatre in 1985. (Photo courtesy of Symphony Society)

SOME WELL KNOWN DANCING TEACHERS

Loraine Goble Loomis
(Source Vickie Wilson)

Marjorie Hall & Emery Greenwell
(Co-instructors) with major contest trophies
(Source - Emery Greenwell)

Pauline Lownes Novo
(Source - Steven Novo)

Audrey Pezzoni Silva
(Source - Audrey Silva)

Vickie Anderson and student
Jennifer Purcell
(Courtesy Vickie Wilson)

"Thats Dancin" 1994
Vickie Anderson Wilson. Students *L-R back row:* Brent
Masterson, Sarah Osborne, Bicanne Weaver and Tommy
Wilson. *Front row:* Joseph Ugalde, Christina Planty, Angel
Ugalde and Jennifer Labastida.

Union Plaza Park Waterfall.

Memorial Plaque at Union Plaza

Lovely Hula Hands - Loraine Loomis Dancers 1957

L-R back row: Linda Kay Corneijo, Valerie Lyman, Karen Arnold, Kathy Dzidzie, Diane Richardson
L-R front row: Jackie Garcia, Nancy Muscio, Paula Harkness, Mary Jo Sesto, Vickie Anderson, Kay Gallant, Carol Peres, Susan Rohde, Joanne
Bell and Cozette Swickard.   (Photo courtesy Vickie Wilson)

A FEW OF SANTA MARIA'S MANY DANCING STYLES

Tap Dancing in the 1940's
(Moore/Coleman Photo)

Mexicana Dancing -1992
Ballet Folklorico of Righetti High School - 1990's
(Photo S&S Enterprises

Above: Folk Dancing at Veterans Memorial Courtyard Audrey Silva, Milton Nichols and Diane Brebes - April 1974. (Photo courtesy Audrey Silva)

Left: Western Dancing - 1992.
(Photo S&S Enterprises)

Bottom Left: Belly Dancing in Elks Rodeo Parade - 1994

Below: "Ballet Bar Work"
(*Santa Maria Times* photo)

SANTA MARIA CIVIC THEATER & PCPA MARIAN THEATER

"The Curious Savage" — 1982. *L-R:* Rosemary Gibson, Diana Bing, Ron Gibson (director), Keith Bing,, Tom Smith. (Photo courtesy Tom Smith)

Santa Maria Civic Theatre, 1660 No. McClelland St. — building bought from Pacific Telephone Co. in 1965 and converted to 100 seat Theatre in the Round. (Photo courtesy Tom Smith)

CIVIC THEATRE

The Santa Maria Civic Theatre is one of the oldest non-professional community theaters on the Central Coast. The group was founded in the living room of Tom and Meg Smith, in October, 1959 when 35 people gathered there in answer to a notice in the newspaper announcing the formation of a live theater in Santa Maria. Among the charter members of the talented group were Hancock College professors, Charles Chenoweth and Gene Ryan; Santa Maria High School teachers, Jan Cresap, Roy Russell and Joe Kunch. During the first season, the theater group expanded to include native Santa Marians, as well as local business people, housewives, agri-growers and engineers from nearby Vandenbergh Air Force Base.

SMCT opened with "The Tender Trap" on the cafetorium stage of the Alvin Ave. School. For the next five years, the talented group performed wherever it could find the space. Scenery and stage props were built in members' garages and rehearsals were held in homes, unoccupied office foyers after business hours and church fellowship halls. Furniture was borrowed from local stores and members sold ads to local business owners to cover program printing costs.

"The Girls in 509" — 1968. *L-R:* Meg Smith, Scotti Temple, Don Sanchez. (Photo courtesy Tom Smith)

"Under the Yum Yum Tree" — 1979. *L-R:* Tom Smith (director), Freddi Weaver (props), Kingston George (lighting dir.), Meg Smith (stage mgr.). (Photo courtesy Tom Smith)

Marian Theatre of Pacific Conservatory of the Performing Arts (PCPA) at Hancock College Campus. (Photo courtesy SMV Chamber of Commerce)

"The Boy Friend" — 1966. *L-R:* Gene Stillwell, Marie Silva, Tom Trevor. (Photo courtesy Audrey Silva)

P.C.P.A

In Summer 1964, Donovan Marley brought his dream of a regional repertory theatre and conservatory to Allan Hancock College. The Platform Players built the Interim Theatre stage in an old barracks building on the north side of the Campus and began the great productions that have continued ever since, totaling over 600 by 1994. 1965-66 was a season of firsts: Its first musical, The Children's Theatre Wagon Circuits, the first starring role for Rosalind Perlman, professional, actress, director and teacher, the first choreographed show by professional dancer Agnes Grogan, and voter-approved $1 million in bonds to build the Marian Theatre Performing Arts Center. P.C.P.A.'s vocation school for actors and stage technicians under the guidance of skilled professionals has been a huge success of great theatre and great training. It is nationally recognized and considered the cultural jewel of the Central Coast. Artistic Director Jack Shouse succeeded Donovan Marley in 1986.

THEATRES AND "THE SPIRIT OF ST. LOUIS"

Studio Theatre — 200 blk. E. Main St. — Grand Opening Oct. 1944. (Moore/Coleman photo)

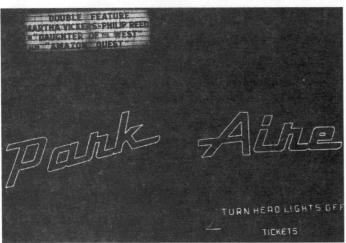

Left: Park Aire Drive-In screen. 200 blk. E. Donovan. Opened June 14, 1949. (Moore/Coleman photo)

Right: Park Aire Drive-In entrance. (Moore/Coleman photo)

Left: Brooks Field Operations Office. The movie "Spirit of St. Louis" converted many old Hancock Airport buildings on Allan Hancock College Campus to photograph the story of Lindberg's famous flight. (Photo courtesy Alice Shimizu Maxon)

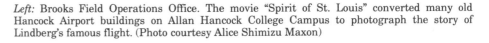

Robertson Aircraft Corp. (Photo courtesy Alice Shmizu Maxon)

Spirit of St. Louis — one of three exact copies built for the movie (in case of accidents) (Photo by Merv Slosson)

NEWSPAPERS, RADIO & TV

Santa Maria Times offices — 1895 — upstairs in T.A. Jones Bldg.

Santa Maria Times FM Radio KRJM — live broadcast of orchestra on stage at Veterans' Memorial Auditorium De Molay Event circa 1948. Sound booth at left. KRJM started in 1947, merged into KSMA in 1949. (Moore/Colman photo).

Santa Maria Times offices — 200 blk. W. Main St. Gold lettering on windows replicates the *Daily Times* and ship masthead of the 1920's and 30's.

New KSMA/KSNI Radio Bldg, Skyway Dr.

KSMA 1240 AM, KNSI 102 FM offices at 110 W. Cypress from 1963 to 1988 when westside redevelopment destroyed building. (Photo courtesy Ken Park)

Alice Bayliss - Owner-mgr KSMA/KSNI

Santa Maria Times offices and plant from 1950's to 1980. NW cor. Chapel and Lincoln Sts. Later PG&E offices.

City Council on TV —1995

Roger Blaemire
Radio KUHL/ KXFM owner mgr.

Santa Maria Times bldg at Airport Industrial Park on Skyway Drive and Industrial Parkway. Socal Gas Co. offices at rear left.

KCOY -TV Channel 12 bldg. — Skyway Drive

SANTA BARBARA COUNTY FAIR (37th AGRICULTURE DISTRICT

Above: The Big Tent. Farming and Industrial Equipment. Early 1950's (Photo courtesy John Bartel)

Below: Moose Ladies refreshment booth circa 1940. *Center L-R:* Nancy Boden Donati, Faye Smith Peterson, Sally Boden Testa. (Moore/Coleman photo)

Above: Carnival Midway — Kids Paradise

Below: Fair Officials — 1976. *L-R:* Bill Luton, Milo Ferini, Vi Buono, Harvey Allen, unidentified, Bob Baker (Secty Mgr.), Dr. Harold Case, (Ringmaster), Clarence Minetti (B.D. President). (Photo courtesy Dr. Case)

Above: Queen R. and Runner- Up — 1992 (Photo courtesy Floyd Snyder)

Below: 1962 featured mission style entrance with king size papier mache Padre. (Photo courtesy Laurel Hogle Kelly)

Above: Ted Bianchi driving Elks Lodge spring wagon. Dr. Harold case at right. (Photo courtesy Dr. Case)

Left: 1962 Maids of Fair "helping". *L-R:* Helen Bucherk, Diane Taber, Jeanne Weissbuch, Sandy Martin.

A FEW MORE LEADING LADIES

Sadie West

Lois Case

Doris Young

Santa Maria Valley has been blessed with a host of smart, attractive, dedicated and active leading ladies. They have quietly played a significant role in guiding the community toward civic, social, cultural and economic advancement. Over the past 50 years feminine achievements have moved from behind the scenes to front row community participation and leadership. Valley women now work and lead admirably on all levels in nearly all fields (no football yet).

The ladies pictured are just a small sampling of the high achieving female leadership not pictured elsewhere in this book, that makes our town and valley such a nice place to live.

Soma F. Baldwin

Trudy Chern

Frances Beaver

Billie Everett

Dr. Victoria Collatz

Doris Lahr

Marjorie C. Martin

Dr. Olga Daiber Howard

Joni L. Gray

Sister Janet Corcoran

Betty Fletcher

Judy Teague

Marilyn Stanley

Vickie Clift

Betty Ranger

Mary Jane Ikola

Alice Patino

Helen Galvan

Shirley Cisneros

Carman Candelaria

Lauri Tamura

Mary Babbitt

Jeane Sparks

Lori Sylvester

Mayor Casey Kyle and Santa Barbara County Fair 1960 Theme Girl Dawn Kurokawa Kamiya.

Guadalupe Buddhist Church — 1991. L-R: Paul Kurukawa, —, Rev. Yanigahara. (Photo courtesy Kawn Kurokawa Kamiya)

Above: Obon Festival 1958, Leroy Park, Guadalupe. *L-R:* Eddie Miyake, Karen Kurokawa, Bette Kurukawa carrying Betty Ann. (Photo courtesy Dawy Kurokawa Kamiya)

Right: 1995 Obon Festival at Santa Maria Fairground Armory.

Above: Traditional Japanese Torii "Gate" at Matsu's Nursery — 1994.

Left: Eagle Scout — 1931 — Paul Kurokawa. (Photo courtesy Dawn Kurokawa Kamiya)

Right: Elks Parade Rodeo Queen Candidates — 1953. Included Alice Shimizu and Virginia Field (Photo courtesy Alice Maxon)

Right: Guadalupe Buddhist Church Picnic at Avila Beach. *L-R:* Marilyn Nakano, Masao Nakano, Tets Furukawa, Ted Aoki, Charles Nakano — 1988. (Photo courtesy Dawn Kurokawa Kamiya)

Below: Actors Olio at Allan Hancock College — 1954. *L-R:* Helen Almonzo, Alice Shimizu, Elizabeth Sainz, Charmain Graham, Pat Stappart, Joan Kihara Gin, Gloria De Soto. (Photo courtesy Alice Maxon)

Above: Japanese Community Center Amateur Show, 1958. *L-R:* Sammy Maenaga, Mutt Yokotake, Shoji Aoyama. (Photo courtesy Dawn Kurokawa Kamiya)

SOME NOTABLE LOCAL PHOTOGRAPHERS

Ted Bianchi

Ralph Adams

Hank Datter

Freddi K. Weaver

Merve Slawson

Vern Houghton

Richard Giachetto

Tom Smith

Luis Escobar

Kei Koga

Clem Gurko

Greg Villegas

Ken Moore

Paul Blumenfeld

Suzanne Blumenfeld

John Demeter

Mary Ellen Schultz

Janett Sainz

Tom Demeter

Douglas Coleman

Left: Movie Star Joan Crawford recognizing Ralph Adams performance. (Photo courtesy Mr. Adams)

Right: Magician Ralph Harry Adams completing sword basket trick as his son Ralph Adams Jr. emerges unscathed from basket on stage at Hollywood Palace 1967. (Photo courtesy Ralph H. Adams)

CECIL B. DeMILLES "THE TEN COMMANDMENTS"

Left: Gateway of the City of the Pharoahs in the Guadalupe Dunes (*Santa Maria Times* clipping)

The Guadalupe Dunes 12 miles west of Santa Maria is where Cecil B. DeMille filmed the silent movie version of "The Ten Commandments in 1923, and where DeMille buried and abandoned one of the largest sets in feature film history — The City of the Pharaoh, with walls that rose 110 feet and sprawled 750 feet in width, its entrance flanked by 21 sphinxes and four 35-foot Pharaoh statues. This Blockbuster production had a profound effect on the people of Guadalupe and Santa Maria, small towns at the time. The 1990's Archaeologists are digging for remains, but folks who were around in 1923 claim that everything was destroyed before burial in the dunes.

Sphinx at Avelino Morganti home on W. Main St. — 1928 with Ernesto De Gasperis family. (Photo courtesy Ernest De Gasperis)

Guadalupe teenagers playing on Sphinx head in dunes — 1927. (Photo courtesy Ernest De Gasperis)

Half buried Sphinx and Jay Openshaw — circa 1935(?) (Photo courtesy Jay Openshaw)

Movies with desert scenes filmed in the Guadalupe Dunes:

1921 - THE SHEIK with Rudolph Valentino
1923 - THE TEN COMMANDMENTS of
       Cecil B. DeMille
1926 - MOROCCO with Marlene Dietrich

Later movies in Santa Maria Valley had aviation themes and utilized Hancock Field and/or Santa Maria Public Airport for:

THE SPIRIT OF ST. LOUIS
1,000 PLANE RAID
THE ROCKETEERS

Right: Gateway to The City of the Pharaohs

GALLISONS FOR THE FINEST

Gallison's Meat Market in 1965. For over half a century the popular choice for tender, juicy, tasty beef barbecue meat. *L-R:* Allen Kemp, Lee DiBacco, George Gallison, Howard Spahn, Joe DuPere, Frank Globish, "Chuck" Larsen. (Photo courtesy Laurel Hogle Kelly)

Mid-Century barbecue cooked on steel grill. (Moore/Coleman photo)

Shriner's barbecue cooked on spits — in mid-40's. (Moore/Coleman photo)

Putting the meat on the spit — a skilled job. (Photo courtesy SMV Chamber of Commerce)

BBQ CAPITAL OF THE WORLD

Barbecuers at Guadalupe — 1940's.
L-R: Ernie Sanders, Charles Campodonico, Gene Martin, Larry Kyle. (Photo courtesy Marjorie Crawford Martin)

Santa Maria style BBQ crew at Jonathan Club Western Stag BBQ Sept. 22, 1967. *L-R:* Bob Nolan, Bob Seavers, Don Darlington, unidentified, Tom Parks, Bill Pryor, Clarence Mahan, Andy Hanson, "Pete" Peterson. (Photo courtesy SMV Chamber of Commerce)

SMV Pioneer Assn. Barbecuers. Nearly sold out at Jim Gamble's "Pumpkin City" fundraiser for the proposed new "Pioneer Park". *L-R:* Albert Novo, Joe Ramirez, Bill Hadsell.

Santa Maria Club BBQ team removing meat from spit and slicing to serve. *L-R:* Larry Kyle, unidentified, Roy Linman, Lou Thompson, Gene Martin, Mart Schneff. (Photo courtesy Marjorie Crawford Martin)

BBQ team of Filipino Community of SM Valley and Vicinity, Inc. They are one of many local non-profit organizations that regularly offer barbecue lunches (traditionally beef, chicken, ribs, salad, beans and toasted & buttered french bread) to raise funds for community benefit programs. Drive down Broadway and take your pick. *L-R:* Flor Mina, Tony Solomon, Orlando Ramiro, Edgar M. Vea, Manuel Vea.

Bank of Santa Maria BBQ team fed the multitudes at opening celebration of "BBQ Hall of Fame" at SMV Historic Museum April 22, 1995. *L-R back row:* Stan Langenbeck, Jeff Cherry, Jim Glines. *Front row:* Dolores Luis, Becky Peterson, Linda Glines, Betty O'Dea.

BARBECUES FOR ALL

Above: Cutters slicing block of top sirloin. (Photo courtesy Chamber of Commerce)

Right: Digging pit for old style BBQ and a start on the swimming pool at Arroyo Grande Methodist Camp. (Photo by Vern Houghton)

Big barbecue facility at Union Oil Co. picnic grounds near Mr. Solomon. Over a million meals barbecued here.

Political Rally BBQ — Waller Park in 1980's

BBQ contest judges check off contestant's product. (Photo courtesy Chamber of Commerce)

Bianchi Family BBQ picnic 1960 — Waller Park. *L-R;* Bill, Ted, Leo, Margaret, John, Woodrow, Kenneth. (Photo courtesy Ted Bianchi)

SANTA MARIA STYLE BARBECUES & HALL OF FAME

Barbecues were widely enjoyed locally from the earliest days of settlement. As Santa Maria grew and prospered, its barbecues attracted visitors who sang its praises when they returned home. The town's expert barbecuers formed teams to travel and lay on Santa Maria style barbecues on request at many distant locations in California and eventually nation-wide. Bob Seavers, Secretary-Manager of the SMV Chamber of Commerce obtained a copyright for the name and recipe for the "Santa Maria Style Barbecue" in 1967. The history of barbecues in Santa Maria is detailed and illustrated in a 1997 book by R.H. Tesene, founder of the SMV Historic Museum's BBQ Hall of Fame.

Above: Beacon Outpost Bar & Restaurant. Next to Richfield Service Station and Airplane Beacon Tower. Famous for its Saturday night barbecues in 1950 & 60's. (Photo courtesy R.H. Tesene)

Below: Music at the Outpost — *L-R:* Carolyn Elder, Barbara Seals, R.H. Tesene (prop.), Mr. and Mrs. "Hoot" Gibson — circa 1955. (Photo courtesy R.H. Tesene)

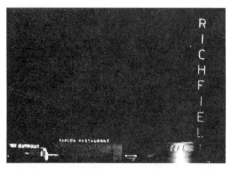

The Outpost, Beacon and Restaurant at night. (Moore/Coleman photo)

SMV Chamber of Commerce lays on barbecue for the State Governor and Legislature, 1967 in Sacramento. *L-R:* Blanche Hobbs, George S. Hobbs, Jr. (SM Mayor), Nancy Reagan, Governor Ronald Reagan, Marty Paulson (Pres. of Chamber of Commerce). (Photo courtesy George Hobbs)

Santa Maria style open air BBQ finger lickin good.

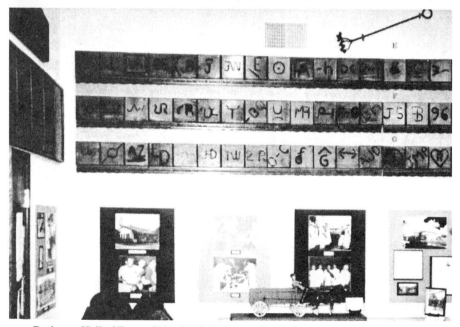

Barbecue Hall of Fame. Gift of R.H. Tesene to SM Valley Historical Society, 1995. (Photo courtesy Mr. Tesene)

Typical weekend Broadway BBQ fundraiser.

KIDS HAVING FUN

Riding bareback. *L-R:* Jeanett Tognazzi (Sainz), Charlotte Tognazzi (Smith), Billy Robbins — 1943 — Los Flores Ranch — Los Alamos. (Photo courtesy Jeanett Sainz)

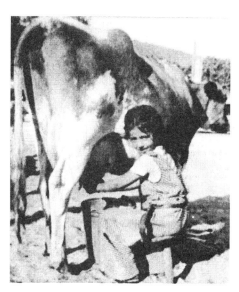

Cow milking — Jeanett L. Tognazzi — 1943 (Photo courtesy Jeanett Sainz)

This pig tail curls to right per young Benjamin R. Lahr. (Photo courtesy Jeanett Sainz)

Right: Bill Lot playing in sand — Avila Beach 1956. (Photo courtesy Patricia Galyan)

Ben Lahr and girl friend in Los Alamos punkin patch. (Photo courtesy Jeanett Sainz)

Cabazon fish caught from rocks at Marre Ranch, Avila. *L-R:* Billy Robbins, Erlinda Pertusi Ontiveros, Charlotte Tognazzi, Jeanett Tognazzi. (Photo courtesy Jeanett Sainz)

Wayne Rasmussen enjoying airplane ride at Pismo Beach Carnival — Summer 1957. (Photo courtesy Patricia Galyan)

Barbara Victorino Snyder in cowgirl costume watching Elks Rodeo parade — circa 1953.

Youthful Elks Parade watcher — 1994

Jr. Criterium Racers. *L-R:* Starter Bob Orach, Lisa Stanford, Stacey Davis, Amanda Rodriguez. (Photo courtesy Floyd Snyder)

SHOOTING, HUNTING & FISHING

Above: Santa Maria's first shooting range (Blue Rock & Rifle) was No. of SM River and E. of 101. Washed out winter 1913-14. *L-R:* Dr. E.K. Dart, Ray Richards, Andy Devine, Willis McMillan, Lawrence Crakes, W.H. "Bill" Crakes, Frank Crakes, Jim Wilson. (Photo courtesy C. Wright Crakes)

Below: Santa Maria's 2nd target range — 1914 to mid century. Four holes in bluff created by bullets passing through targets raised in front still visible from Suey Road river crossing.

Hunters with forked horns — Los Flores Ranch. *L-R:* Larry Lahr, Ben Lahr, Charlie Sainz, Darwin Sainz. (Photo courtesy Jeanett Sainz)

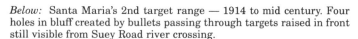

Left: Deep sea fisherman Kai Koga shows off two yellowtail tuna. (Photo courtesy Kai Koga)

Darwin Sainz with four point buck shot on Las Flores Ranch, Las Alamos, 1958. Hung from single tree for dressing and skinning. (Photo courtesy Jeanett Sainz)

Surf fishermen on local beach — : Mas Tony Oyabu, David Navarro, Sonny Ramirez, Leo Gondolfi, Frank Silvera, Bob Garret, Kingo Fukahara, Bert Jakobsen, Miarranna Domingues, Ronnie Oyabu, Francisco Ricolcol. (Photo courtesy Jeanett Sainz)

GOLFERS & GOLF CLUBS

Rancho Maria Golf Club — 1970. *L-R;* Jack O'Keefe, Keith Adams, Jim O'Keefe, Stanley Brown. Holding Tee — Mayor George Hobbs. (Photo courtesy Vennie Lee Brown)

George M. Scott teeing off on opening day of Santa Maria Country Club, circa 1922. Course mostly native grass, weeds & hardpan. (Photo courtesy Richard Weldon)

Above: Twin Sphinx from "The Ten Commandments" guard the entrance to SM Country Club (now Waller Ln.) from the Main Coast Hiway. About 2 miles So. of town. (Postcard courtesy Barbara K. Nelson)

Left: 1953-54 Womens Board — SM Country Club. *L-R:* Mrs. Harold (Maurine) Twyford, Mrs. Phil (Delie) Holmes, Mrs. Paul (Norma) Twyford, Mrs. Charles (Jean) Hoey, Mrs Paul (Sally) Scaroni, Mrs. Martha Lincoln, Phyllis McCuster. (Photo courtesy Dick Weldon)

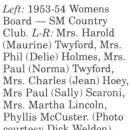

Above: "Cap" Twitchell, Julian Sword and friend on green at SM Country Club. (Photo courtesy Dick Weldon)

Below: Movie star Andy Devine — putting out at SM Country Club circa 1958. Others unidentified. (Photo courtesy Ken Park)

Left: 1988 Cappy Harada Celebrity Golf Tourney — 12th annual. Celebrities include *L-R:* Jim Diani, Charlie Cossa, Hollis Stacy (Lady Pro), Mayor George Hobbs, Cappy Harada, Bob Stowassey. (Photo courtesy George Hobbs)

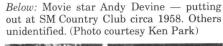

SANTA MARIA INDIANS BASEBALL CLUB

Fifty-two years of semi-pro baseball makes the Indians the oldest semi-pro club in continuous service in California.

The Santa Maria Indians Baseball Club was formed in 1944 by members of Santa Maria's Elks Lodge 1538, succeeding the Santa Maria Merchants team of the 1930's and early 40's.

These Elk leader founders included business manager Manuel Bello and board chairman Frank Shields. Charter members of the original Santa Maria Indians Board of Directors included Dr. A.M. Beekler, B.R. Griffith, E.E. Rubel, Jeff Cochran, Ken Trefts, Larry Lavagnino, Ken Vertrees, Pat Rojas, Lou Thompson, H.E. Terry, Dick Snow, Butch Simas, and Joe Hagerman. Past managers who have contributed their leadership

and baseball knowledge to the development of Indian ball players are Mutt Anderson (1944 season), Butch Simas (1945-60), Rudy Bondietti (1961-73), Rick Pence (1974), John Osborne (1975), Steve McFarland (1976-83;1989), Jim Caveny (1984), Bill Davies (1985-86), Bob Brontsema (1987-88), Matt Stine (1990), Dave Malpass (1991), Tom Benedicht (1992-93), and Doug Noce (1993 -).

In 1950, the tribe defeated a core of Major League All-Stars headed by Cleveland Indian Hall of Famer Bob Lemon.

Since Scoop Nunes took over the reins of the Redmen in 1961, the overall record is 1,315 wins against 321 losses. With this 80% win record, the Tribe is batting an impressive .800.

The Indian's championship resume includes capturing the California State Semi-Professional National Tournament 14 out of 15 years, and a 1979 second place finish at the World Series National Championship in Wichita, Kansas. In 1982, the Tribe won the National Championship at the World Series, the only California team to date to win that honor.

Nineteen ninety-four saw the Indians recapture the NBC State Championship.

The Tribesmen also set a World Series all-time record, hitting the high team average of 405.

Hundreds of local athletes have played on "The Big Red Machine". A few are pictured here.

Leland J. "Butch" Simas
Manager 1945-60

Carl Barbettini
SM Hall of Famer

C.J. "Scoop" Nunes
Gen. Mgr. 1974-96

Billy Wilson

Rick Pense

Mark Arkinson

Craig Ross

Don Gardner

Dave Brunell

Hal Rabourn

Mickey Davis

Milt Guggia

114

SANTA MARIA INDIANS BASEBALL CLUB

1973 Board of Directors fo Santa Maria Indians
L-R: Bob Garioto, Scoop Nunez, Carl Barbettini, John Murray, Larry Lavagnino, (absent - Butch Simas)

Moses Hidalgo

Ariston Julian

John Lizalde

Len Lizalde

Rod Mawhinney

Rene Pili

Hal Province

John Reed

George Vasquez

Robin Baggett

Jay Baker

Mike Mohr

115

SANTA MARIA INDIANS BASEBALL CLUB

Terry Monk

Howard Nickason

Jim Diani

Dick Donati

Jim Draper

Larry Evans

Dean Johnson

Tom Miller

John Renna

Dean Teixeira

Dave Vosburg

Wayne Crabtree

Wes Forman

Jock Osborn

Curt Reade

Frank Reyes

SANTA MARIA INDIANS BASEBALL CLUB

Doak Moore

John Osborn

Bat Boys — 1975
Tony Valozza, Tommy Anderson

Ken Slagle

Terry Lee

Carl Barbettini and
Cappy Harada at the
"Cappy Harada Hot
Stove Dinner"— 1976

Steve McFarland

Doug Nelson

Santa Maria Indian team at the 1976 Wichita National Semi-Pro Championships.

SANTA MARIA LITTLE LEAGUE BASEBALL

Dedication ceremonies for Southside Little League Field to Carl Barbettini at Simas Park — 3-18-95. (Photo Courtesy Vicki Anderson Wilson)

Above: Barbettini Field opening ceremonies. Tommy Wilson, Master of Ceremonies (1st baseman for Tomooka Farms 1994 Champion Team coached by Mike Kelly), greets Mike Maramonte, former Director of Santa Maria's Recreation and Parks Department. (Photo courtesy Vicki Anderson-Wilson)

Right: Orcutt National Little League 1995 District 50 Champions. *Front row L-R:* Ray Jensen, Jasen Sakae, Steve Simpson, Tim Savey. *Middle row:* Mike Kelly, Adam Sweet, Ryan Merlo, Kyle Wilson, Charlie Denham. *Back row:* Ken Bychak, Ryan Smith, Bill Savey, Clint Childress, Chris Woodruff, Jon Strommen, Israel Long, Scott Wilson (Manager). *Not shown:* Bryan Neal and Caleb McCutcheon. (Photo by Luis Escobar)

RIght: The "Catchers". *L-R:* Joe Hagerman, Vernon Simas, Raymond "Mutt" Anderson, Rod Rodenberger, Eddie Anderson. (Photo Vicki Wilson)

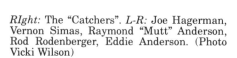

BEAUTIFUL BEACHES

Horseback riding So. of Oceano Beach

Oceano Beach Clamming — view No.

Pismo Beach and Pier. (Photo courtesy Floyd Snyder)

Avila Beach Piers at sunset. (Photo courtesy Floyd Snyder)

Morro Rock Bay and Harbor. (Photo courtesy Floyd Snyder)

Cars still drive on Oceano Beach. (Photo courtesy Floyd Snyder)

Sea Gull at Avila Pier fish cleaning station. (Photo courtesy Ken Park)

Big Pismo Clams were still numerous in 1980.

Southern Sea Otter — cute but endangers Pismo clams' survival. (Photo courtesy Floyd Snyder)

Wind Surfing
(*Santa Maria Times* photo)

119

SANTA MARIA CITY PARKS

Buena Vista Park ....800 S. Pine St.
Memorial Park..............200 N. Pine St.
Simas Park ....500 S. McClelland St.
Preisker Park................2301 Preisker Ln.
Russell Park...................1000 W. Church St.
Adam Park.....................600 W. Enos Dr.
Armstrong Park............1000 E. Chapel St
Atkinson Park...............1000 N. Railroad Ave.
Oakley Park..................1300 N. Western Ave.
Rice Park......................700 E. Sunset Ave.
Tunnell Park.................1100 N. Palisade Dr.
Minami Center ....600 W. Enos Dr.
Central Plaza Park........100 n. Broadway
Joe White Park.............500 S. Palisade Dr.
Alice Trefts Park...........510 E. Park Ave.
Elwyn Mussell Sr. Ctr...510 E. Park
Grogan Park ....1155 W. Rancho Verde
Hagerman Center..........3300 Skyway Dr.
Maramonte Park ....620 E. Sunrise Dr.
Pioneer Park ....1100 W. Foster Rd.

CITY OF GUADALUPE

Leroy Park

SANTA BARBARA COUNTY PARKS

Waller Park....................Bdwy & Goodwin Rd.
Guadalupe Beach ....W. Main St.
Nojoqui Falls Park

PRIVATE PARKS

Camelot Park.................Preisker Ln.
Ikola Historic Park........S. HiWay 101
Illiff Historic Park ....2005 N. Broadway
Mussell Fort..................Tepusquet
Zaca Lake......................Foxen Canyon

RECREATION OF PARKS COMMISSION

1942-43	Hilda Harkness
1942-50	Winifred Crawford
1942	Euland Payne
1942-46	Don Underwood
1942-44	Albert A. Dudley
1942-44	Brett Deveney
1943-44	Hilda Hockett
1944	Andy Wier
1944-46	B.R. Griffith
1944-46	Floyd Watson
1944-4	Fred Anderson
1945-46	Frank Shields
1946-54	Stephen Fairchild
1946-49	Don Taylor
1946	Eugene Bowen
1949-51	E.D. Cochran
1950-81	Alice Trefts
1946-62	Arthur E. Atkinson
1954-58	Carl Engel
1954-76	Karl Bell
1955-93	James "Joe" Hagerman
1958-62	S.F. Larsen
1962-65	Joe R. White
1962-65	Arthur G. Bauer
1962-64	Louis H. Germann
1963	Walter Conrad
1963	John Mudge
1963	Ken Osborn
1964-70	Herbert Von Hammerstein
1965-70	J. Bradley Davenport
1965-68	Ed. J. Zuchelli
1968-70	Thomas B. Urbanske

1970-86	Jack W. Patten
1970-73	Dale P. Kelly
1970-74	Reinhart J. Rabska
1974-86	Dr. Robert C. Miller
1976-93	Marilyn Stanley
1981-94	Ronald J. Rodenberger
1986 —	Henry M. Grennan
1986-88	Robert Orach
1986-94	Herman Kon
1989-94	Michael Rivera
1989-91	Carl Barbettini
1989-90	Willie Galvan
1991-94	Don Hosepian
1991 —	Sister Janet Corcoran
1992 —	Kirk D. Spry
1993-94	Larry G. Tanner
1993 —	Michael Garcia
1983-92	George Haussmann, Jr.
1994 —	Robert Sturgeon

RECREATION AND PARKS

Above: Buena Vista Park with ancient blue gum eucalyptus. (Photo courtesy Ken Park)

Left: Bill Nolan & daughter Nancy feeding ducks & geese at Waller Park — 1948.

Below left: "Mussel Fort" owner-operators Douglas and Audrey Mussell.

Right: Nojoqui Falls — in Springtime. (Photo courtesy Ken Park)

Below left: Recreation & Parks Dept. in historic John & Annie Long house. Built 1885. Exterior remodeled in 1920's.

Below: Joe Hagerman at Santa Maria's 4-field, world class, softball center, (*Santa Maria Times* photo)

Youth Members

1970-71	Steve Consorti
1971-72	Michael hernandez
1972-73	Walter Thad Pentecost
1973-74	James Trowbridge
1974-75	Christine Adam
1975-76	Dale R. Walker
1976-77	Sally Benesh
1977-80	Sheri Benesh
1980-81	Patricia Moran
1981-82	Melinda J. Dennell
1982-85	Jackie Cullivan
1991-93	Michael A. Garcia

Senior Citizen Members

1983-94	George Haussmann, Jr.
1993 —	Marilyn Stanley

SANTA MARIA VALLEY SWIMMING — THE START

Union Oil Company's Bicknell Swimming Pool Grand Opening 1925. First in Santa Maria Valley. (Photo courtesy Pauline Novo)

Girls Swimming Class — Santa Maria Plunge (circa 1950). (Moore/Coleman photo)

Paul Nelson — first city pool mgr. (1925-1952). National Champion Swimmer, Teacher, Coach, leader, inspiration and friend. (Photo from 1933 "Review")

Santa Maria Municipal Plunge. Pool opened 1926 under sponsorship of Santa Maria Kiwanis Club and City. Balcony at upper left. Childrens wading pool at right. Boys swimming class circa 1960. (Moore/Coleman photo)

VALLEY SWIMMING ADVANCES

Santa Maria Plunge; view from Broadway 1930. Landmark water tank at rear. Chamber of Commerce & Historical Museum are now at this location. (Photo courtesy Pauline Novo)

Paul Nelson Pool, opened in 1950. 25 yard competitive section for swimming, diving, water polo and lap swimming.

SMUHS Swim Team 1931. John Paulson swam on U.S. Olympic team at L.A. in 1932. (The Japanese team surprised the U.S. & world with a clean sweep.

North end of Paul Nelson pool, for recreation, classes and practice.

Left: Paul Nelson Pool, dedication plaque.

Right: YMCA pool built in 1980 — recently expanded.

Santa Maria Swim Club — 1983. *Back row L-R:* 7th Brent Briggance, 12th Tara Shriner, 14th Richard Monroe (coach), *3rd row:* 2nd Miriam Hudson, 3rd Cynthia Yee, 4th Wendy Smires, 5th Chris Hajnik, 6th Spencer McCuish, 7th Keoki Briggance, 12th Josh Hudson, 13th Tim Storsteen. *2nd row:* 3rd Sara Hollerbach, 4th Russell Garcia, 6th Marc Hunt, 10th Fred May, 11th Eric Shriner, 13th Michael Yee. *Front row:* 2nd Kathlene Fujinami, 7th Heather Briggance, 10th Kendall Murakami.

GUADALUPE AFTER THE RAILROAD CAME

Southern Pacific Railroad Depot, Guadalupe, Ca. 1892 to 1972. New Amtrack passenger depot to replace circa 1997.

Stephan Campodonico's new brick store. Erected 1884 after fire destroyed entire block of wooden buildings. Many uses over the years, last being "The Muse" night club. Now vacant.

L-R: 2 men unidentified, Dr. J.H. Franklin, Mr. L.D. Waller. In 1912 formed the Waller & Franklin Seed Co., the worlds largest flower seed growers at that time

Guadalupe Jail, Guadalupe Ca. Jail built in 1926. Last used 1966.

1956 aerial view, Cemetery upper left, old fresh vegetable cooler center left, Golden State Creamery, upper right corner: Junction W-166 & Highway 1.

(Note: All photos on this page courtesy Rancho Guadalupe Historical Society)

GUADALUPE — GOOD LIVING

Left: Guadalupe's first fire truck (1920's) in Elks Rodeo Parade 1993. *L-R:* City Councilman Jim Arriola, Fire Chief Henry Lawrence, Mayor Reni Pili with granddaughter, Councilman Richard Pelton.

Guadalupe Rotary-sponsored Rock-etts, 1945 County Softball Champions. *L-R top row:* Melba Nonella, Betty Estes, Barbara Sevier, Bernice Holmes, Olive Hoff, Etta Lee Holmes. *Front row:* Nita Nonella, Barbara Nonella, Dorothy Romero, Edna Nonella, Dorothye Abatti, Mgr. Francis Rojas (not present). (Photo courtesy Betty Silva)

De Gasperis' Butcher Shop — early 1920's. *L-R:* George Juarez, Ernest De Gasperis. (Photo courtesy Merv Slawson)

Guadalupe City Hall — formerly Guadalupe Joint Union School until state earthquake protection laws required new, safer school buildings.

Leroy Park Recreation Pavilion — circa 1948. Alice Shimizu holding Glenn Aoyama. (Photo courtesy Alice S. Maxon)

GUADALUPE — LOTS GOING ON

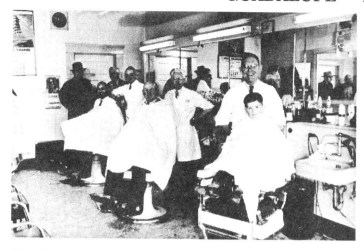

Guadalupe — 3 chair modern barbershop — 1940's — typical of the era in SMV. (Moore/Coleman photo)

Strip-tease artist mingles with enthusiastic guests in Guadalupe nite club in 1940's. Guadalupe, Oceano, and Pismo authorities were more relaxed than straight-laced Santa Maria. (Moore/Coleman photo)

A popular Guadalupe bar with well-dressed patrons in 1940's. (Moore/Coleman photo)

Barbecuers in Guadalupe taking drink break. *L-R:* unidentified, Larry Kyle, Gene Martin, Ernie Sanders (Moore/Coleman photo)

Obon Festival Dancers — inside original Guadalupe Buddhist Church — 1958. *L-R:* Isano Kurukawa, Yoko Yamamoto, Sakaye Minami, Gayle Nakano, Mrs. Ono, Mrs. Iwao and daughter, Joan Kihara Gin, Alice Henmi, Carolyn Eya, Sumi Shimoni, Grace and Jane Araki, Gladys Kitagawa, Elaine Miyamoto, Jean Minami, Dawn Kurokawa, Carolyn Oishi. (Photo courtesy Dawn Kurakawa Kamiya)

GUADALUPE TODAY

Stephen Campodonico Home. Built 1986.
10th & Olivera St.

View No. Guadalupe St. (Hiway 1) from New York Restaurant.

Giacomini Home. Built circa 1900
9th & Olivera St.

Basque House Restaurant & Hotel. Closed. Future uncertain.

One of several City Hall murals depicting
area history.

Colorful wall murals created by students on walls along city entrance E. Main St.

City Hall main entrance

Royal Cinema — out of action after many decades of service

View E. on 10th St. Landmark city water tower at right.

SMALL TOWNS IN SANTA MARIA VALLEY

Garey Store — 1995

Downtown Nipomo — Alex &Jess, a favorite Bar & Barbecue dinner spot in 1941 before Hiway 101 was moved west one mile and business began to move there too. (Photo courtesy Bob & Nancy DeArmond)

Sisquoc Store — 1995

Downtown Nipomo along the coast hiway circa 1941. Knotts Hall, the Knights of Pythias building, and other buildings are long gone. (Photo courtesy Bob & Nancy DeArmond)

Harriston Store — circa 1930. At junction of Hiway 1 and Lompoc Harris Grade Rd. Out of business when Pacific Coast RR station & tracks were removed for salvage during WWII.

Downtown block in Old Orcutt — 1995. Building at right originally Orcutt Post Office, later Mid State Bank until Oak Knolls new bank opened.

Casmalia — 1995. Hitching Post Restaurant

Casmalia Post Office and store — 1995

127

WAR VETERANS REMEMBERED

Left: Santa Maria Veterans Memorial Building.

Below: Bas-Relief in Memorial lobby

Left: Memorial Park.

Memorial Plaque on Park Memorial

54 Made The Ultimate Sacrifice

DIED IN SERVICE WORLD WAR II

Louis Araujo
Charles Baird, Jr.
Glen R. Baker
Ellery Bush
Leonard Calderon
Joseph Carlotti
Charles Carpenter
John H. Capek
Roberta E. Conser
Clarence Cooper
Kenneth Cooper

Nickolas Covel
Joseph D. Coito
Bryant DeLoach
William Dudy
George Elvidge
Augustin N. Escalante
Buford E. Foster
Warham H. Franklin
Fred M. Garton
Ernest F. Gorzel
Frank Golden

Dale Harris
Robert Ireland
William C. Jones
Issac C. Kahn
William Kirkpatrick
Daniel Logan
Robert Longmire
Florentino J. Martinez
Vincent Martinez
Basil Martinez
John McGinley

Ray McGinley
David F. McGraw
Maurice Muxen
Robert W. Neatherlin
Carmen J. Nelson
Thomas Ontiveros
Jack Ontiveros
Christopher Palestino
Fortino M. Rivas
Donald E. Runnels
Dewitt Sanford

Harold Severson
John Donald Smith
Calvin Snow
Gene Sturgeon
Cecil A. Tognazzini
Roy E. Tennison
Stanley Weber
William C. Wallace
Harold Withrow
Mikoto Yoshihara

Attilio De Gasperis — survived first landing on Normandy Beach

Bob Rivers — shot down over Europe. Led successful escape from POW Camp.

Doris Hardisty — President — Wind & W.A.V.E.S. #92.

Left: Interior Courtyard — Vets Memorial

128

VETERANS & ACTIVE MILITARY

Veterans Memorial at Santa Maria Public Cemetery

Disabled American Vets Logo

Ltc. Edward A. Guhl CASMR

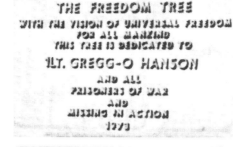

VFW Color Guard

WWII WAVE veterans distributing flags during Desert Shield — Desert Storm campaign. *L-R:* Louise Roberts, Kathryn Tammen, Dorothy Senseney. (Photo courtesy Doris Hardisty)

Lady Marine Vet. Anne Burke

GI Forum Leaders *L-R:* Willie Galvan, Esteban Valenzuela

Capt. Jack A. May — Company Commander DMZ, Panmunjom Korea, on "Bridge of No Return". 1994

Above: Soldiers Sgt. Bob Bouslaugh and Sgt. Wes Maroney at Hafar Al Batin, Saudi Arabia Feb. 15, 1991. (Photo courtesy Wes Maroney)

Below: Tanks on outskirts of Kuwait City in Gulf War — burning oil well at right. (Photo courtesy John K. Fraser)

Commemoration of 50th anniversary of D-Day landings.
Above L-R: Homer Colquitte (VFW soloist), Marvin Douglas, Capt. Raymond A. Champagne, Karen Wilson Grant, VFW Auxiliary Pres., Col. Gordon E. Herb.

Below L-R: Col. David Abella (USAF), Supervisor Mike Stoker, Mayor George S. Hobbs, Judge Barbara Beck, VFW Cmdr. William Pastor, Cmdr. Harley Stonebraker, Katherine Hulme (Museum of Flight Pres.), John E. Smith - WWII vet., *Rear:* Councilman Bob Orach, Ray Rambaugh - American Legion.

Tank Commander 1st Lt. Allan Fraser. Kuwait Dec. 1990. (Photo courtesy Carol Fraser)

VANDENBERG AIR FORCE BASE   WEST COAST MISSILE & SPACE CENTER

VAFB Airport Flight
Control Tower.
(Photo courtesy
Floyd Snyder)

Missile Launch
May 1989

"Slick Six" — launch site planned for space shuttle

Missile for defense of VAFB

Local leaders ready for USAF Nationwide Air Defense Orientation Tour — circa 1984. (USAF photo)

608 days to shuttle launch. Photo Feb. 1984.
Program canceled. It was never launched.

Above: Space shuttle flown in piggy-back on Boeing 747.

Right: USAF cargo plane used to fly in shuttle launch tanks & equipment on display at VAFB.

Dedication of Santa Maria Entrance Gate.
L-R: Gen. Jack Watkins, Joe Sesto, Mayor George Hobbs, Joe Hagerman, George Barnes.

IMPORTANT POLITICAL VISITORS

Left: U.S. Senator Jack Kennedy visit. State Sen. Claire Engle (center) 5th Dist. Supver. Marion A. Smith at left. Circa 1951. (Photo courtesy Marion Smith)

Right: Republican Congressional Leader Newt Gingrich with Congressman Tom Bordonaro. (Photo courtesy Floyd Snyder)

Mayor George Hobbs & U.S. Senator Gary Hart

Republican Leaders visit — 1994. *L-R:* Senator Wm. Bennett, Congresswoman Andrea Seastrand, 4th Dist. County Supervisor Tom Staffel, Mrs. Staffel. (Photo courtesy Floyd Snyder)

Congressman Bob Lagomarsino, Mrs. Lagomarsino, Judge Barbara Beck (at left). Veterans Day dinner.

Governor George Deukmejian visit — 1982. *L-R:* Host Stanley Brown, Carol Hallett (State Assemblywoman), Vennie Lee Brown, Gov. Deukmejian. (Photo courtesy Vennie Lee Brown)

Mayor George Hobbs and Congressional Candidate Michael Huffington (right) at City Hall. (Photo courtesy Floyd Snyder)

State officials. *Sitting L-R:* Brian Setencich - Assbly Spkr, Tom Bordonaro - Assemblyman, Chuck Quackenbush - Insurance Commissioner. Local leaders *L-R:* Joe Prandini, Tony Cossa, Jim Pollard. (Photo Courtesy Floyd Snyder)

President George Bush. Admirers Barbara Snyder and Michael Garcia.

State Senator Jack O'Connell

Congressman Eric Seastrand at groundbreaking with Katherine Hulme & Dan Hoback. (Photo courtesy Wes Kemp)

131

PEOPLE, PLACES & EVENTS

Noontime Kiwanis Club Annual Pancake Breakfast Fundraiser. *L-R:* George Crosby, Ed Ritchie, Sue Moats, and Barbara Snyder (customer).

Santa Maria's famous Golden Dukes semi-pro basketball team (precursor to NBA teams) played standing room only for years. *Top L-R:* Coach Hop Finley, Bob McCutcheon, Sherman Nearman, Madison Stanford, Marv Bergstrom, Chuck Cluska, Robert Hirsch, Duke Webster (sponsor). *Front:* 13-Joe White, 12-Ken Milo, 15-Bill Bertka, 24-Quentin Sims, 11-Gus Rischer, 21-Omer Meeker. (Photo courtesy Joe White)

SM Valley Lions Club White Cane Day Fundraiser. *L-R:* Madeline McEwen, Anika Mathewson — 1995.

Left: Lester Webber. First local athlete to make the majors. Pitched for Brooklyn Dodgers and Cleveland Indians. (Photo courtesy Scoop Nunes)

Right: Local hero Robin Ventura — Golden Glover for Chicago White Sox signing autographs for fans. (Photo courtesy Floyd Snyder)

Ted Bianchi's 1924 Hudson sport convertible roadster. (Photo courtesy Ted Bianchi)

Above: Olympic double gold medalist Mike Larabee (400 meter run) with pets. (*SM Times* photo)

Below: Butch Reynolds — Cribbage Grand Master, National & World Champ — 1980's. (*SM Times* photo)

Left: Fred May — 2nd in U.S. age group Judo. Gold Medal on Japan tour

Right: 1984 Olympic Torch Run Broadway & Newlove Dr

DENNIS BETHEL AND ASSOCIATES

DENNIS BETHEL
(1942 - 1993)

FOUNDER

Dennis Bethel graduated in 1972 with a Bachelor of Architecture from California Polytechnic State University at San Luis Obispo. He obtained his Civil Engineering License. Over the past 18 years, Mr. Bethel was responsible for the planning, design, engineering and processing of hundreds of residential, commercial and industrial land development projects throughout Santa Barbara and San Luis Obispo Counties.

In the Fall of 1980, Mr Bethel started Dennis Bethel & Assoc. to provide consulting services for land development and public works projects in San Luis Obispo and Santa Barbara Counties. He served as Principal for the Company until his death in November of 1993. He also started Urban Planning Concepts in 1987 to provide a land use and environmental consulting services for the Central Coast projects.

Mr. Bethel was also active in local professional and civic organizations including the American Public Works Assoc., California Land Surveyors Assoc., California Council of Civil Engineers and Land Surveyors, City of Santa Maria Chamber of Commerce, campaign committees, and local youth athletic programs.

Mr. Bethel worked on numerous development projects in his 18 years of service in the community resulting in thousands of new homes in Santa Maria. Here is a partial list of his successful projects . . .

Las Brisas	Riviera Estates	Autumnwoods
Cameo Gardens	Emerald Park	Oak Hill Country Estates
Sierra Vista	Deerfield Estates	Oakridge Condos
S.M. Airport Dist.	Tiffany Park	Elkhorn Estates
Country Club Estates	Betteravia Government Center	Rancho Verde
Westridge	Bayview Estates	Woodmere
LandCo	Town Center Mall	Southpoint
Northpoint	Crystal Creek	Terrace Park
First Assembly of God Church	Cottages on the Green	Knightbridge
Quail Meadows	Foxenwood Country Club Estates	
Regency Estates	Kimberly Place	

SANTA MARIA BERRY FARMS / SHEEHY BERRY FARMS — 52 GREAT YEARS!

Terrance Sheehy

Robert Sheehy

1470 E. Stowell Road
P.O. Box 1946
Santa Maria, California 93456

Santa Maria Berry Farms was established in SM Valley in 1944 by Kenneth and Rod Sheehy. It was the first commercial strawberry farm in the valley. It started with 60 acres. In 1951 they established Sheehy Berry Farms as successor. Kenneth Sheehy passed away in 1953 and Roderick Sheehy passed away in 1956. Robert and Terrance Sheehy assumed management control in 1956.

Innovative and aggressive, the Sheehys shipped the first load of strawberries out of Santa Maria by air. The cargo was flown in a World War II C-46 Curtis Commando operated by Flying Tiger Airlines from Hancock Field to Chicago. Demand for Sheehy's high quality strawberries grew steadily. Today they supply a world-wide market by air from Los Angeles via major airlines to all parts of Europe, Asia and the Middle East.

Santa Maria Berry Farms also pioneered rail shipment of strawberries from Santa Maria. They perfected cooling techniques that permitted shipments to markets all over the United States. In 1962 Sheehy's switched to 100% truck transportation for U.S. deliveries because of faster deliveries and better cooling provided by trucks.

In 1984 Terrance Sheehy became the sole proprietor of Sheehy Berry Farms. His son Brian and daughter Mary Ellen joined him as equal partners.

Santa Maria Berry Farms is now owned and operated by Robert Sheehy and his two sons, Robby and Pat.

The Sheehy Berry Farms have been affiliated with Driscoll Strawberry Association since 1951. All of their strawberry plants are especially bred in Northern California, are patented and cannot be used by anyone not a member of Driscoll.

Early office

COAST ROCK PRODUCTS — FOUNDED 1956 BY JAKE WILL

Jake Will

Jake Will came to Santa Maria Valley in 1941 to survey and layout Camp Cooke. After completion he was hired by S.P. Milling Co. to manage a ready-mix operation being set up to supply concrete around-the-clock for building roads, barracks and other facilities at the Camp.

In 1942 Jake moved the ready-mix plant to the Santa Maria Air Base at the corner of Blosser Rd. and McCoy Lane. It supplied concrete for runways, aprons, and hangars for P-38 fighter planes, and for oilfields, and Santa Maria city growth during and after the war.

Jake became President of SP Milling Co. but in 1956 resigned and founded Coast Rock Products. He bought land near town on E. Donovon Rd. near Suey Park and erected a concrete batch plant. At the same time he leased from Capt. G. Allen Hancock land near the Garey Bridge on the Sisquoc River to mine and process aggregate.

Today, Coast Rock and its affiliate companies, owned in part by the Hermreck Family, serves the Central Coast from King City to Santa Barbara, and continues its forty years of significant impacts on construction throughout the region.

Right: Ready Mix Truck Fleet Coast Rock. Photo 1958.

CUSTOM COLORS

Our new location — 315 Dal Porto Lane

Where it began — 1730 So. Broadway. (1985 photo)

Custom Colors

AND AUTO BODY SUPPLIES, INC.

315 WEST DAL PORTO LANE ● SANTA MARIA

Custom Colors Auto Body Supplies, Inc. opened it's doors 23 years ago. It was first established in 1965 as Mathews Plating and Supply, a combination automotive paint and headstone business. In 1972 Bob Tuck, a long time car painter and thereafter a manager of Mathews Plating, bought the existing business located a 1930 S. Broadway and renamed it. In 1979 Custom Colors, now a family affair with Bob and his 2 sons Alan & Dean, began selling strictly automotive paints and supplies.

The 80's saw a steady growth in the demand for automotive paint and supplies and with this Custom Colors' 2,000 square foot store could no longer handle the business load. Needing a larger and more functional up to date facility, Bob opened the doors in 1990 to a new 6,500 square foot building located at 315 W. Dal Porto Lane. Four years later Bob sold Custom Colors to his oldest son, Alan, who had been involved in the business since 1975.

The 90's have seen drastic changes in the automotive painting industry. Custom Colors has met the challenge by carrying only top quality paints such as DuPont, BASF and Nason, 3M products and a full range of related supplies and equipment. In addition, providing computerized color matching, VOC tracking and equipment repair are just a few of the other ways Custom Colors has shown their ongoing dedication to customer service.

AGRO-JAL FARMS

Home Grown Success of *Agro-Jal Farms*

The Maldonado family has been farming in the Santa Maria valley since 1965. Maldonado Sr. began working for Adams Farms and developed a reputation that led Jack Adams to call him "the best employee I've ever had". The hard work that earned that praise was applied to their first humble 3 acre parcel in 1977 with a co-op farm venture. By 1967, with the applied efforts of his entire family he resigned his position with Adams farms and began farming 50 acres of strawberries on their own. Abel Maldonado Jr., after completing his studies in 1988 at Cal Poly SLO, returned to assist in the family farm operation. That year Abel negotiated an additional 180 acres with the intention of growing broccoli and cauliflower, as well as incorporating as Agro-Jal Farms. During 1988, Agro-Jal Farms, Inc. introduced its' first strawberry label, "Red-Diamonds." The amount of land leased for farm production by the company now totaled 180 acres in vegetables and 96 acres in berries. In 1990, they introduced their second strawberry label as "Paloma" (Dove). During this year the total number of vegetable acres leased for production increased to 230, and the berry acreage remained at 96 acres. Early in 1991, Agro-Jal Farms, Inc. purchased a 5.25 acre industrial parcel on West Main with the future intentions of developing a corporate office and cooler plant. By 1993, they were able to realize their dream of their own cooler with the aid of a loan from Mid-State Bank and Central Coast Development Corporation who arranged an SBA loan.

Agro-Jal Farms, Inc. has shown steady growth in leased land and increased profitability. In 1992 they negotiated 2 large land leases adding nearly 900 acres to their totals. One of the main reasons that Agro-Jal Farms, Inc. has been so successful is because the <u>entire family is so dedicated to their work.</u> Maldonado Sr. brings 30 years of farming and field management. He has implemented the majority of the company standards regarding crop production, crop rotation, and labor duties and responsibilities in the company fields. His numerous years of personal experience in all the above mentioned related areas offer tremendous benefits to the other family members along with all the employees. He also has brought valuable personal standards with his work ethic for the other family members and employees to follow.

Abel Jr. has worked on the family farm since early in elementary school. Although he is only 29 years old at this writing, he has over 18 years of farming experience. His father has taught him all the aspects of farming. He brought new management ideas to their farming operation that has greatly enhanced the profitability. Abel Jr. has largely been responsible for much of the negotiation of the most recent land acquisitions. The idea to expand the farm operation into shipping was also Abel's. On a personal note, Abel's love and concern for his town prompted him to run for and secure a seat on the city council in 1994. At the time of this writing he is pursuing the mayoral seat. There may be a post script after November 5th.

Abel's siblings, 26 year old twins Frank and Patty are also major factors in the company's success. Frank has worked on the family farms since a young boy. He also has the benefit of having learned all the important skills that are necessary to manage this large of a farm operation. His extensive background greatly assists his father with all the production and labor related jobs necessary to successfully control the company field operation. Patty, the only Maldonado daughter, also plays a tremendously important part in this company. Her sales and computer skills allow her to control all the computer data base, handle payroll, maintain daily income and expense data for accounting purposes, etc., moreover assist Abel with the office management need daily. Also their mother Gloria, is the company receptionist and secretary.

The key to Agro-Jal Farms' success has been honesty, hard work, loyalty, and their father, Maldonado Sr. Agro-Jal Farms as a corporation only started in 1988, and since that time they have increased the size of their operation from 230 acres to 1400 acres. It was in 1992 that the company began to distribute and sell its own produce. Agro-Jal Farms, Inc. began with only a few buyers then, and now have over 120 customers nationally. It was not easy getting into the distribution of their produce but now that people have had the opportunity to see the consistent quality and packaging of the Agro-Jal berries and vegetables produce, "they buy again and again from us". As a company, Agro-Jal Farms emphasizes that we do the growing, the packing, and the shipping so that we have control of our product from the field to placing it on the truck. After several years with the Paloma and Red-Diamond labels being on the streets throughout much of the United States, Agro-Jal Farms has a reputation of providing their customers with a consistent quality product and service.

In 1995 Agro-Jal Farms, Inc. was recognized by the Strawberry Growers Association as the Sales Organization of the Year. Abel Jr. actively represents our area in the California Strawberry Growers Association. 1995 also found Agro-Jal with the opportunity to purchase their first acreage, a 535 acre ranch near Sisquoc. This ranch was a portion of the historic Newhall ranch. With this acquisition, Agro-Jal Farms solidified their presence in the farming community and early in 1996 they completed and moved into their new corporate offices adjoining their cooler. The Maldonado family has demonstrated that the American dream of success for immigrants to this country is still possible.

by Eric Gamble

Original Dudley Mortuary on So. Lincoln & Church Sts. (SE Corner)

New Dudley—Hoffman Mortuary on E. Stowell Road.

DUDLEY—HOFFMAN
MORTUARY

The firm was founded in 1876 by T.A. Jones and his son Samuel Jefferson Jones. Originally the business was called "T.A. Jones & Son, Furniture & Undertaker". In 1904 Albert A. Dudley became associated with them as a mortician and purchased the undertaking part of the business in 1914, changing the name to Dudley Mortuary.

In 1930 Mr. Dudley sold his business to his son Russell, managing the firm until 1960, when he purchased the business.

In 1972 he was joined by his son, Jeffrey E. Hoffman, who now manages the business. In 1979 the Hoffman's added a Crematory and Columbarium. They now have a full staff of professional personnel to help with all needs of the community.

THE GAS COMPANY

1907-1941

We're Proud to be a Player in the City of Santa Maria's History

Santa Maria Gas Company merged with Southern Counties Gas Company in the early forties. At the time Santa Maria Gas Co. had the distinction of being the oldest distributor of natural gas in the state. It was founded by two Santa Maria bankers, James F. Goodwin and Paul Tietzen at the turn of the century. In 1970 Southern Counties merged with Southern California Gas Company as we know it today. Approximately 3, 000 Santa Maria homes enjoyed the benefits of gas in 1941. Today over 30,000 homes are served.

We are pleased to be part of the City's history and "GLAD TO BE OF SERVICE".

1941-1970

ROEMERS

The Roemer family began serving farm and ranch owners in 1890 when Joseph Roemer, father of Frank R. and Alfred E., founded a blacksmith shop at Bdwy. and Chapel.

In 1916 Frank and Alfred formed "Roemer and Roemer". It included blacksmithing, farm implements, automobiles, woodwork and manufacturing school bus bodies. Early in WWI, it had 57 employees. A 1921 fire destroyed the building. A new one was built at Bdwy. and Mill. In the early 20's, the firm dissolved and Frank formed Valley Motor Sales, joining Rubel Motors to sell Buicks. Alfred carried on the original business. Wm. Elliott became a partner. The firm expanded into pump and implement sales, known separately as "Roemer and Elliott".

In 1939, Glenn Roemer, son of Alfred, bought "Roemer and Roemer" and operated it under his own name. The firm installed and serviced dairy equipment throughout the Central Coast and sold general hardware and farm supplies.

In 1977, Vard A. Roemer and Robert R. Roemer, sons of Glenn, bought the firm and still operate "Roemers" ant its branches along the Central Coast plus a nationally distributed mail-order catalog. They sell western wear, veterinary supplies, saddles and tack, fencing products, feed and livestock supplements, and all other farm and ranch supplies.

For four generations of 106 years, the Roemer family has served well its farm and ranch customers and the public.

SANTA MARIA VALLEY RAILROAD COMPANY
(SMVRR) SINCE 1911

The SMVRR was built and incorporated in 1911 by Santa Maria Oilfields of California, Inc., an English syndicate.

Capt. G Allan Hancock purchased the Railroad at a Sheriff's Auction on the steps of the Santa Barbara Courthouse in 1925. He reorganized the vitalized the property by building a new engine house, an office building, buying new locomotives and upgrading the track and roadbed.

SMVRR continues to play an important role in the economy of Santa Maria Valley, hauling petroleum, potatoes, liquid plastics, and other important bulk cargo.

Top Left: THEN: 1925 — Steam Locomotive

Left: NOW: 1995 — Modern Diesel Locomotive

THE DIANI FAMILY

Lorenzo Diani, born on October 15, 1882 in Figione, Switzerland emigrated to America in 1920 with his wife the former Mary Dolinda Balzani. After a short stay in San Francisco they soon moved south to Greenfield, California where he worked at a dairy. In 1928 the Diani's moved to the Santa Maria Valley to the community of Betteravia to operate, in partnership, a dairy with the Union Sugar Company. In 1939 they bought out Union Sugar's share and moved to a farm west of Santa Maria.

Lorenzo and Mary raised two children, A.J. and Madeline. Madeline married into the Bianchi family (Woodrow) and worked for Union Sugar Company for 43 years. A.J. after serv-

ing 3½ years in the Navy during World War II, formed A.J. Diani Construction Co., Inc. in 1949, which exists today under the ownership of sons Bob, Jim and Mike and son in-law Don Ward. A.J. bought the Santa Maria Club in 1981, which today is the Landmark Square and was a founding board member of the Bank of Santa Maria and has served as Chairman of the Board since its inception.

A.J. and the former Margaret Bowden of New Zealand raised five children. Cecilia (Teixeira), Bob, Susan (Ward) Jim and Mike. All the children were born at Sisters Hospital, attended local schools and reside in the area. There are currently 14 grandchildren and 2 great grandchildren.

INDEX

INDEX

INDEX